Attachment Infused Addiction Treatment®

(AIAT)

When Vodka Makes More Sense Than People

Mary Crocker Cook, Ph.D., D.Min., LMFT, LAADC

Attachment Infused Addiction Treatment®

Copyright © 2025 Mary Crocker Cook

ISBN: 978-1-61170-332-0

Published by:

RₚP **Robertson Publishing**™
www.RobertsonPublishing.com

Printed in the USA and UK on acid-free paper.

Dedication

I am deeply grateful to the faculty of the San Jose´ City College Alcohol and Drug Studies Program who supported, and even pushed, me to take the sabbatical I needed to complete my text. I could not have done this without Demetria Iacocca, Jose Flores, Pauline Casper, and Franci Kendrick. I am a better person because of you.

Love, Mary

Contents

Section Two: Treatment Application of the Attachment Infused Addiction Model® (AIAT)

Chapter One

Chapter Two

Chapter Three

Chapter Four

Chapter Five

Introduction

The Attachment Infused Addiction Treatment® (AIAT) model is based on a simple proposal: individuals develop a secure attachment to substances to self-soothe in the absence of available caretakers. While the use of substances is a reliable strategy that makes sense to the user, addiction hijacks the individual's ability to form effective self-regulation skills and utilize support to achieve long-term sobriety. It is the foundation of this model that individuals who have experienced substantial attachment disruption are unable to utilize the traditional structure of addiction treatment and Twelve Step culture. This population, with their accompanying trauma, requires an approach that directly addresses this attachment disruption within the addiction treatment structure and staff. Recovering clients will need extensive assistance to gain self-regulation skills they can employ both individually and with others, and this includes strengthening their internal observer. They must develop the skills to accurately reflect on their own internal reality, and accurately reflect the reality of others. A large part of their treatment will include an intentional development of a social network as part of relapse prevention planning, with frequent reflection on their own attachment style and how their currently attachment strategies may or may not be effective with the others in the treatment milieu as well as staff. This approach requires more transparency from the staff, as they will need to model strong reflexive function skills. These individuals desperately need to be accurately seen and heard.

Attachment Infused Addiction Treatment® (AIAT) is also a response to my professional quest, decades long, to create a clinical bridge between the mental health clinician culture and substance use counselor culture. As a professional that stands astride both specialties, I have often felt as though I had to speak from only one side of my professional experience based on the audience I might be addressing. The schism in cultures creates holes in our treatment planning, disharmony in treatment settings, and most importantly leads to disjointed and ineffective treatment for the isolated, suffering addict.

What links mental health and substance use cultures is early attachment theory and Edward Khantzian's Self-Medication Hypothesis[1]; his insight that *addiction is pain relieving instead of pleasure seeking*. The psychological pain, and eventually physical pain, is temporarily suspended by substances which means that he sees addiction as a self-regulation disorder. Often substance-based self-regulation patterns were developed in response to a trauma-based attachment interruption, and all Attachment Infused Addiction Treatment® needs to be offered in trauma-informed settings. Trauma-informed systems and services take into account knowledge about trauma—its impact, interpersonal dynamics, and paths to recovery—and incorporate this knowledge thoroughly in all aspects of service delivery.

In the process of these attempts to self-regulate with substances, the adaptation in brain circuitry and neurophysiology is altered in a way that the brain functioning of the substance abuser is permanently changed. Prolonged use of substances can alter neural synapses and the endogenous production of certain neurotransmitters that affect the reward center of the brain. In addition to the neurological changes of addiction, chronic stress leads to dysregulation of our stress hormones – which leads to unregulated inflammation. When we experience stressful emotions – anger, fear, worry, anxiety, rumination, grief, loss – the HPA axis releases stress hormones, including cortisol and inflammatory cytokines that promote inflammation. Inflammation translates into symptoms and disease that follows us well into adulthood. According to the "Theory of Everything", your emotional biography becomes your physical biology, which is why there is a significant link between individuals who experience chronic stress and significantly higher levels of inflammation and disease.

The Attachment Infused Addiction Treatment® model situates the physical and psychological pain in un-remediated attachment interruption, which traps recovering clients in a hyperarousal or hypo-arousal neurological response, resulting in an inability to self-soothe or receive soothing from external resources. In the process of attempting to manage attachment threats with substances, clients are neurologically hijacked and develop the disease of addiction. Individuals who experience disorganized, avoidant, or anxious attachment in infancy develop difficulties in reflecting on their own thoughts and accurately reading the thoughts and intentions of others. This impaired ability prevents substance abusing clients from effectively identifying and interrupting their self-harming patterns. It also prevents them from fully utilizing the counseling, family and community support that research demonstrates are crucial for long-term recovery. This difficulty can lead to an increasingly discouraging relapse cycle.

The Attachment Infused Addiction Treatment® model provides a persuasive argument for the resulting emotional regulation possible when individuals: (a) understand what causes addiction (biochemistry and early attachment disruption), (b) draw from interpersonal neurology to stabilize neurological flooding to address an overactive inflammatory system, (c) identify attachment styles and attachment strategies, (d) learn to recognize risk factors for relapse (cravings, environmental cues, and disruptive attachment strategies and defenses in relationships), and (e) develop tools for coping with stressful situations (increasing ability to establish and maintain secure attachments to support metacognitive strategies and utilize recovery tools learned in treatment).

In a perfect world, we would accomplish these goals with staffing comprised of licensed attachment-based therapists, attachment-trained addiction counselors, psychiatrists, an internal medicine physician, peer counselors, and somatic therapists and naturopathic medicine in addition to medication-assisted treatment when necessary to manage cravings. In reality, most of us work in county facilities and non-profit contracted agencies, and the staffing options are more limited. It was important to me to develop a model of treatment that would utilize the resources most likely available.

Section One:
Theory of Attachment-Infused Addiction Treatment®

Chapter One

1.1 The Role of Attachment

Affective states cannot be completely regulated by individuals themselves as "we all are emotional regulators of each other."[2]

John Bowlby devoted extensive research to the concept of attachment, describing it as a "lasting psychological connectedness between human beings."[3] A *secure* attachment bond ensures that a child will feel secure, understood, and calm enough to experience optimal development of his or her nervous system. The child's developing brain organizes itself to provide the child with the best foundation for life: a feeling of safety that results in eagerness to learn, healthy self-awareness, trust, and empathy. An infant develops a secure emotional attachment to the caregiver who fosters a child's secure attachment soon after the child begins to show distress or cries by holding or cuddling the infant and toddler in ways that are noticeably comforting to the child.

The caregiver with whom a child develops a secure attachment sees and hears the child accurately. The caregiver learns correctly to understand, interpret, and then appropriately react to the child's behavior. This adult behavior establishes within an infant and toddler a felt knowledge that the youngster's behavior is respected, interesting, and significant to the caregiver.

"Secure attachment is hypothesized to promote expectations that others will be responsive to their needs thereby developing a perception of self-efficacy in dealing with challenges and a willingness to seek support from others during times of distress."[4] The caregivers' acceptance of the child's emotions as well as their ability and willingness to openly communicate about them, encourages emotional awareness and self-regulation in the child. The neurobiological and psychological regulatory effects of attachment are either immediate – when the attachment figure influences emotional responding directly (e.g., by hugging a crying child) – or more generalized – when mental representations of the attachment figure are used.[5]

Clinicians like Mary Ainsworth point out the parent's ability to accept protest without retaliation or excessive anxiety is also a key determinant of secure attachment. The child must be welcomed back with unconditional intimacy. Parents m**ust resolve their own attachment needs to tolerate the child's growing need to differentiate** (establish a "self" apart from the parent). A child needs empathic attunement from parental figures to develop a cohesive self.

In line with this, researchers such as Liable &Thompson[6], mothers of securely attached children are not only more sensitive to their child's emotions, but they also tend to communicate with their child in a richer and more elaborative manner and to be more supportive and validating towards the child's point of view while actively coaching emotion regulation. In this way, they encourage the child to develop a better understanding of the psychological mechanisms (including the role of emotions) in human interactions and other everyday experiences, which allows the child to develop a greater social competence

1.2 Internal Working Models

The caregiver provides a set of experiences that set up an internal working model of attachment. The internal working model is the brain's way of making a summation of experience. To anticipate future action, it has to summarize past events. It is natural for the brain to summarize. The model stays with the child throughout the child's life and is totally changeable. The model changes when the experience changes, thus the word "working."

These internal working models are conceived as operational models of self and attachment partner, based on their joint relationship history. They serve to regulate, interpret, and predict both the attachment figures and the self's attachment-related behavior, thoughts, and feelings.

A working model of self as valued and competent, according to this view, is constructed in the context of a working model of parents as emotionally available, but also supportive of exploratory activities. Conversely, a working model of self as devalued and incompetent is the counterpart of a working model of parents as rejecting or ignoring of attachment behavior and/or interfering with exploration. Thus, the developing complementary models of self and parents taken together represent both sides of the relationship.[8]

In the internal working model, the parent's sensitivity to the infant's signals determines how the infant will respond. This requires that the parent demonstrate:

- awareness of the signals
- the ability to interpret their meanings
- an appropriate response in a timely manner.

Mary Ainsworth defined parental sensitivity as the ability of a caregiver to be aware of the signals the baby sends, and the meaning of the signals for what is going on inside of the child. **Mentalization** is the ability to recognize that someone else has a mind different from one's own. It involves the ability to infer someone else's mind by facial expression, tone of voice and non-verbal communication. It involves the neurological areas concerned with action imitation, face imitation and intention understanding. Ainsworth said that the parent is tuning into the mind of the child and can talk about the inner nature of the child.[9]

Highly self-reflective parents, Fonagy et al.[10] maintain, are better able to see a situation from their infant's perspective, to empathize with their infant's emotions, and hence to respond to the infant's attachment signals with caring behavior that successfully meets the infant's needs for comforting. Evidence suggests that the capacity for what Fonagy calls Reflexive Self Functioning (RSF), the capacity for mentalizing, can develop only in a secure attachment relationship where the child does not have to be preoccupied with the availability or well-being of the mother.

The relationship between Reflexive Self Functioning (RSF) and substance abuse has been described as a two-way process by Allen, Fonagy and Bateman.[11] Substance abuse and intoxication weakens RSF, both in relation to understanding oneself, and in relation to giving attention to the mental states of others.[12] On the other hand, weakened or impaired "baseline RSF" may contribute to frustration and high emotional arousal, which in turn is often resolved by using substances. The latter implies that substance abuse also can be viewed as a clinical expression for weakened RSF and accompanying problems with affect regulation.[13]

Mentalization happens through the mirror neuron system - a group of specialized neurons that "mirrors" the actions and behavior of others. The involvement of mirror neuron system (MNS) is implicated in neurocognitive functions (social cognition, language, empathy, theory of mind) and neuropsychiatric disorders. Parental attunement and mirroring have been documented on a physiological level as well. The heart rates of securely attached infants and their mothers in the Ainsworth's "Strange Situation" parallel each other, whereas they do not with insecurely attached infants and their mothers.[14] The mirroring of heart rates indicates the mother's sensitivity and involvement in her infant's perceived experience. Mothers of secure infants pick their babies up more quickly when they show signs of distress, play with them more, and generally seem more aware of them and their needs than parents of insecure infants.

The blurring of self and other representations may be a critical mechanism through which the brain achieves what Tomasello and colleagues call 'shared intentionality'.[15] Shared intentionality refers to the sharing of psychological states between individuals and is intimately connected to joint attention, cooperative communication, collaborative action and instructed learning. Tomasello and colleagues suggest in turn that these capacities for shared intentionality, joint attention and cooperative behaviors were critical stepping-stones toward the evolution of altruistic behavior in humans.

Secure attachment is associated with an internalized sense of lovability, of being worthy of care, of being effective in eliciting care when required, and a sense of personal efficacy in dealing with most stressors independently. Secure preschoolers develop an understanding of other people's thoughts and emotions, leading to empathy. An internal working model of the world as responsive and available for re-engagement allows for "emotion-focused coping"[16] that enables the acknowledgement and expression of feelings, as well as the seeking of emotional support, so that distress can be reduced. This in turn enables the successful use of "problem-focused coping" and therefore creates a constructive way of coping.[17] *Security, one might say, is the capacity to directly, flexibly, creatively, and actively engage in the solution of interpersonal and intrapsychic attachment problems as they arise.*

Fritz Heider noted that when we react to other people, we do not usually perceive their actions as movement patterns that have to be laboriously interpreted. Rather, we understand others' behaviors (i.e., we construct working models) in terms of how others make us feel, and what we believe them to be intending, thinking, perceiving and feeling.[18]

Adults generally make such inferences rapidly, relying on familiar patterns in the situation. This includes not only the other person's emotional expressions and the situational context, but also knowledge of past interactions (drawing on working models). What distinguishes children's from adults' internal working models is the complexity of the attribution-making and meaning-making involved.

In fact, one distinction between infant–caregiver versus adult attachment bonds is the notion of interdependence. Although infants are highly dependent upon caregivers for emotional and physiological support, caregivers are not similarly dependent upon infants. By contrast, adults in attachment relationships frequently require emotional support from one another. Within the attachment framework, a great emphasis upon perceived responsiveness in times of need or stress is common to both infant–caregiver and adult attachment literatures.[19,20,21] However, the complexity of interdependence that characterizes adult attachment relationships suggests important differences in how adults manage attachment relationships.

Mutuality in interdependent relationships empowers the relationship by bringing clarity, directness, and predictability to the thoughts, feelings, and intentions of the individuals who inhabit them. *In fact, a sign of a secure reflexive self-reflection is the ability to self-regulate well enough to share the narrative of their lives in a collaborative, balanced manner.* There is no unconscious need to alter the narrative to create a positive impression, and there are no intrusive thoughts that substantially derail the conversation. Mutuality manifests as a genuine interest in fostering growth in one's relational partner, an interest that is perceived to be reciprocal.[22]

1.3 Attachment Theory in the Cultural Context

I wanted to briefly address the cultural context for Attachment Theory and acknowledge that while Margaret Main conducted her original "Strange Situation" studies in Uganda, the majority of research has been conducted in the US, Europe, and the UK. The entire premise of attachment theory is based on the idea that the attachment bond is an evolved behavior system, which makes it a universal human construct. This means that as a species, all humans, regardless of cultural context, are genetically predisposed to develop an attachment to a caregiver during infancy. After some debate on whether attachment truly exists in all cultures, there is now consensus that the attachment behavioral system is applicable to and present in all humans.[23]

The above is considered the universality hypothesis of attachment theory, which suggests that attachment security patterns are consistent across all cultures with the secure type being the superior, preferred type of attachment and insecure types being the deviant or non-preferred types that occur in the presence of multiple risk factors in the environment.[24] Conversely, some researchers who propose a more culturally sensitive version of attachment theory suggest that some insecure attachment behaviors may be positively adaptive responses to specific contextual and cultural antecedents in the same way that secure attachment behaviors are contextually adaptive.[25] Crittenden, in particular, prefers the term **strategies** for the insecure attachment styles, and I will be incorporating this terminology in the AIAT® model. Both views emphasize the importance of sensitive care from the primary caregiver and the existence of specific infant secure-base (i.e., exploratory and proximity-seeking) behaviors, but disagree as to how these behaviors are measured and interpreted in relation to culture.

The idea that attachment style varies by cultural context also maps onto recent work on attachment security's situational dependence. Attachment style is generally thought of as a stable personality dimension or dispositional trait. However, attachment style is based on internal working models that reflect life experiences, *implying that changes in life experiences can cause some fluctuation in attachment security*. Indeed, recent research shows that attachment can vary according to context in a way that is largely unrelated to a person's dispositional attachment style. For instance, priming different attachment mindsets or reminding people of times when they felt secure or insecure can activate specific attachment schemata and even influence attachment-related behavior.[26] This will be important in conceptualizing recovery in a broad, community context. Recovery does not happen in isolation, and great effort will be made to shift the attachment from the substance to attachment to people. One of the final exercises in completing the treatment protocol will be the completion of a social network map in preparation for program completion. This supports the view of addiction as a chronic condition with the need for ongoing support.

A recently developed state adult attachment measure provides further evidence that attachment style varies across time and situations.[27] The influence of ongoing events on attachment security supports the prediction that culture, a broad and pervasive context, influences attachment.

Chapter Two

2.1 Interpersonal Neurology: Brain Integration as the Basis of Secure Attachment

SCIENCE ALERT!!!

This next section is important, and I know "science dense." While I tend to nerd out on neurology, I know this is not everyone's jam. However, the physicality of the consequences of interrupted attachment is key to guiding the intervention we use, so I encourage you to devote time here and understand it well enough to be able to describe what is happening to your clients in non-jargon ways. For example, *"When we come from unpredictable and traumatic environments, our brain spends all its time watching the external environment to be safe. So, relationships aren't seen as helpful or safe – probably are the threat. We don't learn to manage the inside of us - our reactions - because we are managing the external world to survive."*

Here is what is happening neurologically:

- Interpersonal Neurologist Daniel Seigel. M.D.[28] states that the integrative regions of the brain include the:Cerebellum: coordinates bodily movement, integrating emotion with thought

- Middle prefrontal area: dorsal and ventral medial prefrontal cortex, the orbital frontal cortex, the prefrontal lateral ventral cortex and anterial cingulate

- Corpus colosseum: linking the left and right hemispheres

- Hippocampus – profoundly integrative for memory, context, emotional regulation.

These are the areas damaged during trauma, abuse, neglect and are **very sensitive to the cortisol surges that happen when we feel threatened in our relationships and environment**. Relationships may support the growth of these areas, which means that integrative relationships grow these areas of the brain.

Interpersonal neurobiology explains the development of the human mind within a social context in which the right brain is encoded and matures through relationship with another brain.[29,30,31,32]

Affect regulation theory teaches that the **earliest form of memory is implicit, bodily based, and cocreated by the mother–infant dyad**.

Thus, the "relational unconscious" and the "social unconscious" are encoded in the right, nonverbal, subcortical region of the brain—what Schore calls "the biological substrate" of the human unconscious. Panksepp and Biven assert that all "raw emotional feelings, instinctual emotional behaviors, and accompanying visceral responses are orchestrated by . . . distinct subcortical systems."[33] This helps us understand why we can be "reactive" in situations with other people when our logic would tell us we are safe. This is not frontal lobe, conscious material. In fact, is non-verbal and sensory which is why we often address emotional regulation through non-verbal and somatic exercise rather than a CBT worksheet!

The prefrontal cortex coordinates and balances the body, brain stem, cortex and limbic system, and integrates it. It also attunes you with other people, balances your emotions, and modulates fear response, flexibility, insight (knowing how your past connects to your present and your future,) empathy, and morality in how we relate to one another. The prefrontal lobe allows us to learn the emotional regulation skills now that we may not have learned with our original caretaker. The key is to eventually align the limbic and prefrontal areas through an integrative approach, so we are more often choosing our responses rather than reacting.

Brain Integration is the basis of secure attachment

Integrative communication stimulates the activity and growth of integrative fibers of the brain between sensory and prefrontal areas of the brain. *Self-regulation of attention, emotion, memory and behavior are dependent on integration, and integration permits the coordination and balance of a relationship nervous system.*

The outcome of integration is regulation. Every aspect of the brain that is involved in affect and attention regulation are integrative regions. When integration is impaired, you get chaos (hyperarousal) or rigidity (hypo arousal) and you can propose that chaos and rigidity should predict impairments in integrated structures in the brain.

In *The Science of the Art of Psychotherapy*[34], Allan Schore states, *"My studies in affective and developmental neuroscience have suggested that the adaptive survival functions of the right hemisphere, the "locus of emotional brain," are dominant in relational contexts at all stages of the life span, including the intimate context of psychotherapy."*

2.2 Attachment Strategies

Attachment strategies for regulating emotional arousal are conceptualized on a continuum as styles of protected and defensive processes.[35] The preferred strategies for regulating arousal are thought to be activated by the perception of danger, which usually takes the form of attachment threat, that is a fear of rejection or abandonment, or an attempt to humiliate. When caretakers are unavailable, children may develop a defensive strategy of dismissing or excluding certain emotions and experiences and **primarily trust cognition to "read" a relational situation**. Alternatively, when caregivers are unpredictable, children may use coercive or clinging strategies and **primarily trust emotion to "read" a relational situation**. In either strategy, our cognition and emotions are no longer aligned, impeding our ability to accurately "read" the internal reality of ourselves and others.

Additionally, when early caregivers are not available to provide the emotional regulation that we need, we don't develop internalized mental representations, or an internal picture, to reassure ourselves when becoming distressed, like remembering the sound of our mother's voice or the way she would hug us. We must either develop anxious behavioral strategies to force a response from the environment, which will not always be soothing, or develop avoidance strategies to remain in denial of our need for soothing. When someone becomes addicted, Philip Flores says, mechanisms for healthy attachment are "hijacked," resulting in dependence on addictive substances or behaviors. *Flores believes that addicts, even before their addiction kicks in, struggle knowing how to form emotional bonds to connect to other people.*

2.3 De-activating Strategies

When attachment security is disrupted or inhibited, the activation of other important behavioral systems (e.g., exploration, caregiving, sociability) is also impaired.[36]

When timely and accurate response to distress is unavailable or met with rejection, the attempts at attachment can be deactivated. The resulting deactivating strategies[37] aim to avoid the distress and frustration caused by the unavailability of the attachment figure. Hearing "no" is so painful we learn to stop asking. Therefore, we inhibit the seeking of support and focus on self-reliance and may cling to "things" because we find people too threatening. We may focus on activity or intellectual development rather than the people around us because people increase our anxiety and distress. This creates a greater vulnerability to process addictions, such as gambling or theft.

When attachment needs are consequently denied, closeness, intimacy, and dependence on others are avoided. Furthermore, continued and generalized distancing (symbolical as well as literal) from distress is achieved through an active inattention to vulnerabilities and threats, including the suppression and inhibition of related memories or thoughts.[38] We may not even recognize the increase in stress, even though our heart rate may be rising, or we may feel restless. **We have learned to tune out our physical cues**. Researchers conceptualize the avoidant, or dismissive, stance in terms of **deactivation of the attachment system**. Anything that would normally activate the system, such as physical or psychological threats to the self, feelings of vulnerability, or wishes for an attachment figure's protection or support, is defended against, suppressed, countered with narcissistic self-enhancement (grandiosity), or denied. [39,40,41]

The avoidant stance is encouraged by: (a) consistent inattention, rejection, or angry disapproval on the part of an attachment figure in response to a person's bids for proximity (closeness) and support; (b) threats of punishment or rejection if the person makes a bid for proximity, intimacy, or protection; (c) traumatic or abusive experiences during proximity-seeking efforts; and (d) explicit or implicit encouragement on the part of an attachment figure for one's greater self-reliance and suppression of expressions of need or vulnerability.

Any experience of internal comfort or safety comes from our ability to comfort ourselves, solve the problem alone, and any praise would come in response to our over-sized independence and self-reliance. Because WE are overwhelmed by the experience of strong emotions, we assume that others would experience our emotions as a "trauma dump" even if we were expressing a preference or disagreeing! Our instinct when threatened would be to get busy or withdraw until we feel more stable.

2.4 Activating Strategies

When the availability of an actual or symbolic attachment figure is intermittent and unreliable, we remain in a state of distress and attachment insecurity. Our focus remains on attempts to be seen and heard accurately, and efforts to reach that goal are intensified via hyper acti-vating strategies.[42] These strategies result in constant concern, vigi-lance and efforts at connections to solicit soothing. This includes strong attempts (e.g., clinging and controlling) to **force** care, closeness, and affection. Therefore, hyper activating strategies reflect a compromise between the anger directed at unavailable attachment figures and the intense need to be close to them.[43]

People who apply these hyper activating strategies often perceive us as incompetent (e.g., at emotion regulation) and helpless[44], and we also develop an overdependence on our attachment figure.[45] Further-more, the neurological excitatory pathways involved in these strategies lead to hypervigilance regarding possible threats to the self and the unavailability of the attachment figure. **We are hyper focused on THEIR availability and responses, and not on our own.** This is why we can be so oblivious to our effect on other people.

Anxious hyperarousal activated in response to unreliable or unre-sponsive care includes ineffective regulation of distress and construing ourselves as inadequately supported, insufficiently loved, vulnerable to uncontrollable threats, and improperly or unfairly treated. In this state of mind, our attention is focused on our own vulnerability and inadequacy in the threatening situation, which seems very real. ("I'm hopelessly alone," "I'm worthless") and/or raged against ("He's never there for me," "She promised me this would never happen"). This state of mind encourages anxiety, rumination, catastrophizing, jealousy, and envy, and can lead to increased efforts to capture a relationship part-ner's attention and loyalty (by acting seductive, being coy, submitting to otherwise undesirable requests) and/or to attempts to coerce the part-ner into behaving more supportively (by making demands, expressing strong negative feelings, denigrating rivals, or spying on the partner).

The anxious stance or state of mind is encouraged by (a) unreliable care, being sometimes affectionate and at other times neglectful; (b) intrusive care that is more related to the caregiver's own needs and anx-ieties than the needs of the attached individual; (c) care that discour-ages the acquisition of self-regulation skills and, directly or indirectly, punishes a person for attempting to function independently; (d) com-ments that emphasize a person's helplessness, incompetence, or weak-ness when trying to operate autonomously; and traumatic or abusive experiences endured when one is separated from attachment figures.

This kind of treatment causes us to feel ambivalent because, on the one hand, relying on the attachment figure is awkward, discomforting, and sometimes annoying, but on the other hand, trying to take care of ourselves can seem dangerous or hopeless and therefore daunting. Unpredictable care may encourage us to verbalize neediness and protest temporary abandonment, real or imagined, because making noise has sometimes recaptured a neglectful or self-preoccupied caregiver's attention. It could force the parent or partner to respond, even if the response was not comforting. Any response feels less distressing than no response. *This encourages inauthentic emotionality*, a form of behavior that can be humorous or endearing but that can also seem dishonest and become exhausting for anyone who tries to respond helpfully to it.

Because closeness and attention from the caregiver, once obtained, is often not soothing and may be punishing, we remain persistently anxious and angry. In response to the intermittent reinforcement for turning to the attachment figure for security, the need to be vigilant for her presence and loss is strongly reinforced. *Our confidence in ourselves to respond appropriately to threats and self-soothe does not develop adequately*, as all of our coping mechanisms are being developed to manage external threats to security.

2.5 Disorganized Strategies

Later attachment theorists found an approach/avoid attempt to attach to caregivers that forms when terrified by the caregiver. We have attachment circuitry in our brain that says that *when I am upset, my attachment figure should soothe me.* But if the caregivers are terrifying to you and you experience terror, then the circuits of fight, flight or freeze get triggered to get away from the caregiver. Both circuits are simultaneously activated which is a biological paradox. *It is experienced as fear without a solution, leading to dissociation for survival. We are trapped in fear without a solution.*

Most insecure state of mind, disorganized attachment, seems to stem from experiences with an attachment figure who was either seriously abusive or "frightened or frightening" when we sought proximity (closeness) and safety from the attachment.[46,47] Mothers of disorganized babies were observed to loom in the child's face, talking too loudly, approaching the child too quickly or suddenly, threatening the child, or being outright abusive.

These experiences turn what should have been a safe haven and secure base into a source of threat, causing all organized attachment strategies to break down. Thus, our biologically based tendency to turn to the attachment figure in times of trouble is countered by the biologically based tendency to turn away from threat, and we are literally stuck. In childhood, these incompatible tendencies lead to unusual behavior – lying down on the floor in the middle of seeking proximity, veering off course when approaching the parent and going under a table, backing away from the parent while in obvious distress, freezing. In adulthood, the equivalent state can involve odd beliefs, dissociative states, extreme lack of trust in others, and, when discussing loss or trauma, a lack of monitoring of discourse or reasoning.

Main and her associates found that parents of disorganized children often have trauma or unresolved loss in their histories. *Particular behaviors of the child may trigger unresolved trauma or loss in the parent and thereby activate fear and/or dissociation in the mother in ways that are sudden and out of context for the child.* [48] The child is likely to become frightened and experience the caregiver as a source of fear.

We can often become confused by others' intentions towards us, as we struggle to connect their behavior with their intent and might frequently attribute negative meaning and intent in their communications with us, which can be very puzzling to them! It is hard for us to take communication from others at face value, creating chaos in our primary relationships with others. We literally "don't understand" what people mean when they are attempting to connect with us and can become frightened. We need to learn to read context cues and read people more literally and learn to stay in our body and not dissociate when threatened so we can negotiate our relationships more successfully.

2.6 Role of Polyvagal Theory

We now have a neural explanation for this "freezing" or dissociative response to threat which can give us insight into intervention with dysregulated emotional systems. One nerve is of particular interest to Dr. Stephen Porges, Ph.D. Dr. Porges is a distinguished university lecturer, scientist, and developer of what is referred to as "polyvagal theory." The vagus nerve is the tenth cranial nerve, a very long and wandering nerve that begins at the medulla oblongata, a part of the brain located in the lower part of the brain just above where the brain connects with our spinal cord.

There are two sides to this vagus nerve, the dorsal (back) and the ventral (front). From there, the two sides of the vagus nerve run down throughout our body. They are considered to have the widest distribution of nerves within the human body.

In polyvagal theory, Dr. Porges describes the process in which our neural circuits read cues of danger in our environment as neuroception. Through this process of neuroception, we are experiencing the world in a way in which we are involuntarily scanning situations and people to determine if they are safe or dangerous. Neuroception answers the question, "In this moment am I safe or in danger?" The autonomic nervous system moves into the state that brings the energy needed to manage the situation effectively.

As part of our autonomic nervous system, this process is happening without us being aware of it. Just as we can breathe without having to intentionally tell ourselves to take a breath, we are able to scan our environment for cues without telling ourselves to do so.

The vagus nerve is of particular interest during this process of neuroception. In the process of neuroception, both sides of our vagus nerve can be stimulated. Each side (ventral and dorsal) has been found to respond in distinct ways as we scan and process information from our environment and social interactions.

The ventral side of the vagus nerve responds to cues of safety in our environment and interactions. It supports feelings of physical safety and safe emotional connection to others in our social environment.

The dorsal side of the vagus nerve responds to cues of danger. It pulls us away from connection, out of awareness, and into a state of self-protection. In moments when we might experience a cue of extreme danger, we can shut down and feel frozen, an indication that our dorsal vagus nerve has taken over.

The branches of the vagus nerve serve different evolutionary stress responses in mammals: the more primitive branch elicits immobilization behaviors (e.g., feigning death), whereas the more evolved branch is linked to social communication and self-soothing behaviors. These functions follow a hierarchy, where the most primitive systems are activated only when the more evolved functions fail. These neural pathways regulate autonomic state and the expression of emotional and social behavior. Thus, according to this theory, physiological state dictates the range of behavior and psychological experience. Polyvagal theory is an allows us to understand the physical anatomy of the dissociative response.[49]

- Within his polyvagal theory, Porges describes the three evolutionary stages involved in the development of our autonomic nervous system. Rather than simply suggesting that there is a balance between our sympathetic and parasympathetic nervous systems, Porges describes a hierarchy of responses built into our autonomic nervous**immobilization.** Described as the oldest pathway, this involves an immobilization response. As you might remember, the dorsal side of the vagus nerve responds to cues of extreme danger, causing us to become immobile. This causes us to respond to fear by becoming frozen, numb, and shutting down. It is almost as if our parasympathetic nervous system is kicking into overdrive as our response causes us to freeze rather than simply slow down.

- **Mobilization.** Within this response, we tapped into our sympathetic nervous system which helps us mobilize in the face of a danger cue. We spring into action with our adrenaline rush to get away from danger or to fight off our threat. Polyvagal theory suggests this pathway was next to develop in the evolutionary hierarchy.

- **Social engagement.** The newest addition to the hierarchy of responses is based on the ventral (front) side of the vagus nerve. This part of the vagus nerve responds to feelings of safety and connection. Social engagement allows us to feel anchored, which is facilitated by that ventral vagus pathway. In this space, we can feel safe, calm, connected, and engaged.

Another way to think about this is that the autonomic nervous system works in a predictable hierarchy.

At the top of the hierarchy is **ventral vagus**; the state of safety and connection. When we are confronted with a challenge that overwhelms the capacity of our ventral vagus (social vagal) system moves into regulation, we move down into the **mobilization** of the sympathetic nervous system, and some form of fight or flight. And if that doesn't resolve the challenge, the final move is to the bottom of the hierarchy – the immobilization and disconnection of the dorsal vagus system.

The ability to successfully adapt to the changing environment relies on the autonomic nervous system's ability to respond and recover.

As humans, we are constantly scanning the environment around us for safety and danger. And, according to polyvagal theory, the way our nervous system perceives threats impacts how our brain and body will respond to the situation. When we are experiencing excess immobilization or are seeing danger cues more often than we should, it may be helpful to work on exercises to calm the vagus nerve. Ways to calm the vagus nerves are mostly physical, including meditation, exercise, and breathing exercises. Psychotherapy may also be helpful, especially if your "fight, flight, or freeze" response may be overactive due to past trauma.

Why does this matter? The different insecure states of mind have implications for the kinds of defensive behavior a person is likely to exhibit.

People who score high on avoidant attachment tend to be vigilant about becoming needy, intimate, dependent, or emotional; they deny vulnerability, emphasize their personal strengths, avoid threats, and resist becoming dependent on anyone.

People who score high in attachment anxiety, in contrast, tend to be vigilant about possible neglect, rejection, or abandonment and be hypersensitive to signs of danger and lack of care. This can either cause them to act out noisily and intrusively or to comply submissively with relationship partners' requests. If necessary, to gain support they will admit – and perhaps even exaggerate – their own weaknesses and vulnerabilities. That is, whereas avoidant people are worried about intimacy, engulfment, and interdependence, anxious people are worried about separation, abandonment, isolation, and interpersonal distance.

Disorganized people may react to others with excessive anger or fear in situations that would not normally elicit this intense reaction. They are frequently confused in social situations, often accusing others of negative intent.

1. Maunder and Hunter[50] summarize the influence of hyperactivating and deactivating strategies (i.e., secondary attachment strategies, as described in more detail above) as a general vulnerability factor for substance abuse in three ways: First, insecure attachment is accompanied by a heightened susceptibility to and a more pronounced physiological response to stressful events.

2. Second, it is accompanied by less efficient methods for emotion regulation, including a preferred use of external methods (e.g., substance use).

3. Third, it is accompanied by less effective and less frequent help-seeking behavior.

While it is commonly understood that early childhood attachments to parents and family are necessary for healthy development, Flores says, emotional attachments remain necessary throughout adulthood. It's not enough, he says, to "just stop drinking."[51] To achieve long-term well-being, addicts need opportunities to forge healthy emotional attachments. ***Theorist Reading[52] elegantly proposes that the client and therapist need to appreciate and understand together how addiction has served as a bond that replaced affectional bonds.***

There is evidence that substance abuse affects attachment as well. The consequences of substance abuse are a host of well-known developmental risks and neurological impairments. From an attachment perspective, four mental processes might be directly affected by substance abuse.[53]

- First, exploration of the environment is reduced or distorted, or risks are taken that would never have been taken in a state of sobriety.

- Second, mentalization, *the exploration of the inner, mental world of oneself and others* is reduced. This might even be a possible motivation for substance abuse: non-mentalization and nonperception of distress and painful memories.

- Third, age-appropriate experiences in relationships often are inhibited or even prevented.

- Fourth, affect regulation and reward might be replaced by substance abuse system.

Chapter Three

3.1 Our Immune System Under the Stress of Interrupted Attachment

This next section was included because, over the years, I have worked with so many people who have manifested their lives through their bodies because they were not processing their experience through language. As we have learned, attachment strategies that focus on external threats to attachment have left many of us unable to accurately read ourselves and others. It is very likely our body has its own story it could tell us, and our history is encoded in our cells if not easily accessed directly through memory. I wanted to provide some information about the impact of this pattern on our immune system.

Children who experience early attachment disruptions with their caregivers are more likely to experience addiction to illicit drugs as adults. Studies have shown that childhood adversity influences all stages of addiction from initiation of drug consumption to long-term maintenance of the addicted state. Adverse childhood experiences can also influence the innate immune system and trigger an immune response. The immune system continues to develop after birth, which is influenced by the postnatal environment such as psychosocial stress in childhood.

The immune system is the body's master operating control system. What happens in the brain in childhood sets up lifelong programming for this master operating system governing all: body, brain, mind. The unifying principle of this new "theory of everything" is that your emotional biography becomes your physical biology. And together they write much of the script for how you will live your life.

Lets' say your immune system has to fight a viral or bacterial infection. Lots of white blood cells charge to the site of the infection. Those white blood cells secrete inflammatory cytokines to help destroy the infiltrating pathogens and repair damaged tissues. However, when those cytokines aren't well regulated, or become too great in number, rather than repair tissue they cause tissue damage.

When we experience stressful emotions – anger, fear, worry, anxiety, rumination, grief, loss – the HPA axis releases stress hormones, including cortisol and inflammatory cytokines, that promote inflammation.

More subtle types of tissue damage can happen slowly over time, in response to chronic stress. When your system is repeatedly overstimulated, it begins to downshift in response to stress. This downshifting creates an inability to access our internal reality over time, impairing our ability to communicate our needs and wants accurately. When you review the drawing below, it becomes clear that our body and emotions are integrated, even when we have trained ourselves to "ignore" physical cues. The system is operating like a car stuck in acceleration without relief.

Excess stress does not always show up as the "feeling" of being stressed. Many stresses go directly into our physical body and may only be recognized by the physical symptoms we manifest. Two excellent examples of stress induced conditions are "eye twitching" and "teeth-grinding." Conversely, we may "feel" lots of emotional stress in our emotional body and have very few physical symptoms or signs in our body. We are not experiencing an integrated message either way.

But remember, this stress response is supposed to react to a big stressor, pump into defensive action, and then quickly recover and return to a state of quiet homeostasis, relaxing into rest and recovery. *You see the bear, run from the bear, and he either eats you or you escape!* The problem is, when you are facing a lot of chronic stress, the stress response never shuts off. You're caught, perpetually, in the first half of the stress cycle. *The bear is circling you over and over again*. There is no state of recovery. Instead, the stress response is always mildly on – pumping out a chronic low dose of inflammatory chemicals. The stress glands – the hypothalamus, the HPA axis – secrete low levels of stress hormones all the time, leading to chronic cytokine activity and inflammation.

Chronic stress leads to dysregulation of our stress hormones – which leads to unregulated inflammation. And inflammation translates into symptoms and disease. This is why there is a significant link between individuals who experience chronic stress and significantly higher levels of inflammation and disease.

3.2 Mending the Body through the Gut

Recent science shows that a sophisticated neural network transmits messages from trillions of digestive bacteria to the brain, exerting a powerful influence on our state of mind – **creating a feedback loop**

between the brain and the gut that goes both ways. Emotional adversity, mental stress, and trauma lead to a greater proliferation of bad bacteria in the gut. Bad bugs in the gut lead to lower mood, anxiety, depression, and a proclivity for being less resilient in the face of adversity and stress.

Why?

Firstly, gut bacteria manufacture more than 80 percent of the body's supply of serotonin, which significantly influences mood. And second, good gut macrobiotics such as those found in probiotics have a direct effect on neurotransmitter receptors in the brain such as GABA.

The messages between the gut and the brain are transmitted via the vagus nerve – which is a primary mediator of the inflammatory stress response. Your vagus nerve conveys sensory information about the conditions inside your gut from your enteric nervous system to your brain. In response, it conveys motor signals from your brain to your gut. We visited the motor reactions when we explored the polyvagal theory! That's why scientists have begun to refer to our gut as "the second brain." The gut microbiome heavily influences neural development, brain chemistry, emotional behavior, pain perception, learning and memory.

Because microorganisms in our gut control our brain, we need to do whatever we can to make our microbiome healthy and give the pathways in our brain all the serotonin and nutrients they need to send the correct messages along our brain's synapses.

Why does this matter? When our early attachment was disrupted, we learned to overinterpret and rely on feelings, or on our intellect. In both cases, we have not learned to "read" our physical cues accurately which impairs our ability to regulate ourselves and address our distress accurately. *It can be an easier beginning of the regulation process to start with nutritional and physical interventions,* like stretching and yoga, while you develop your skills to read yourself and others more accurately.

3.3 Lifespan Changes in Stress Response

Changes to our lifelong stress response happen through a process known as **epigenetics.** Epigenetic changes occur when early environmental influences both good (nurturing caregivers, a healthy diet, clean air and water) and bad (stressful conditions, poor diet, infections or harmful chemicals) permanently alter which genes become active in the body.

These epigenetic shifts take place due to a process called gene methylation. Our DNA is not just sitting there. It's wrapped up very tightly and coated to protect proteins, which together make up the chromosome. It doesn't matter what your genome is; what matters is how your genome is expressed. And for genes to be expressed properly, the chromosome has to be unwound and opened up, like a flower, right at that particular gene.

Margaret McCarthy, Ph.D. Maryland School of Medicine describes it this way. *"You're watching a flower bloom, and as it opens up, it's covered with blemishes."* She folds several of her fingers back in, as if they're suddenly unable to budge. *"Those blemishes keep it from flourishing as it otherwise would. If, when our DNA opens up, it's covered with these methylation marks, that gene can't express itself properly in the way that it should."*[54]

When such epigenetic silencing occurs, McCarthy continues, these small chemical markers – also known as methyl groups – adhere to specific genes that are supposed to govern the activity of stress hormone receptors in our brain. These chemical markers silence important genes in the segment of our genome that oversees our hippocampus's regulation of stress hormones in adulthood.

When the brain can't moderate our biological response, it goes into a state of constant hyperarousal and reactivity. Inflammatory hormones and chemicals keep coursing through your body at the slightest provocation.

This long-term change creates a new physiological set point for how active our endocrine and immune function will churn out a damaging cocktail of stress neurochemicals that barrage our bodies and cells when we're thirty, forty, fifty, and beyond. We are always responding.

Dr. McCarthy offers this analogy: *"Imagine for a moment that your body receives its stress hormones and chemicals through an IV drip that's turned on high when needed. And when the crisis passes, it's switched off again. Now think of it this way: kids whose brains have undergone epigenetic changes because of early adversity have an inflammation-promoting drip of fight-or-flight hormones turned on high every day – and there is no off switch.*[55]

If we had early trauma, our adult HPA stress axis can't distinguish between real danger and perceived stress.

Dan Seigel[56] states that experience changes epigenetic changes in genes. It also turns out that you can inherit the epigenetic changes in genetic molecules created by experience from your parents and grandparents. **You do pass on changes, not in the sequencing of genes, but epigenetic changes due to experience.**

We need to study how psychotherapy shifts the epigenetic changes in our clients. There has been some research that looks at the HPA axis, which is responsible for releasing cortisol hormone under stress. If you have been abused, the HPA stress response is shifted in the brain, making us more vulnerable to future stressors. **The question is how does psychology shift this HPA axis for our clients to create epigenetic changes in our clients to increase their resilience?**

Neurobiological research has focused on motivational processes of both attachment and substance abuse [57] Both are transmitted by the same mesolimbic and mesocortical circuits, and for both, dopamine, endorphins, oxytocin, and vasopressin play important roles. This line of research mainly relies on the reward–deficiency hypothesis of addiction[58].

Assuming that psychotropic substances can substitute other "deficient" sources of reward, attachment theory posits that insecure individuals have not sufficiently experienced the reward of a secure base. Their reward system tends to be insufficiently conditioned to satisfaction by social contact. They assume that insecure attachment and insufficient conditioning to reward by social contact leads to a lack of endorphins in the VTA. As a consequence, dopaminergic reward processing in the limbic system cannot be released. **This leads to a DOPAMINE REWARD INSUFFUCIENCY and increases the risk for addictive behaviors.** Gabor Mate has posited that opioids might be an especially a potent substitute for lacking attachment strategies as it enhances the endorphin system and has described the feeling of a high as a "warm hug."

Recently, Alvarez-Monjaras et al.[60] have presented a multifactorial developmental model of attachment and addiction. The model basically assumes a functional interchangeability of attachment processes and substance use. **According to this model, positive attachment experiences and secure patterns strengthen reward from social contact and**

decrease the risk for addictive behaviors. Negative attachment experiences and insecurity, on the other hand, lead to insufficient reward from social contact and to a heightened risk to replace it with addictive behavior.

3.4 Neuroconnectivity

Attachment theory holds that just as a biological intervention like medication will alter behavior, environmental interventions such as secure attachments produce alterations in an individual's neurology and biochemistry. *The theory states that our emotions and neurophysiology are an open feedback loop, which requires input and external regulation from attachment figures.* **We cannot independently regulate our own affect in childhood.**

"At birth we are biologically waiting for input from adults around us to 'serve and return,' a back and forth interaction that literally shapes the architecture of the infant brain," report Dr. Jack Shonkoff, M.D., Director of Harvard's Center on the Developing Child and his colleagues in a 2012 video "The Science of Neglect" [61] "It begins when a child looks at something, observers something, that's the "serve." The "return" is when the parent responds to the child. When serve and return is broken, you literally are pulling away the essential ingredients for the development of human brain architecture..."

When a baby is not attended to, that is a sign of danger to the baby's biological systems, so its stress systems are activated. In a brain that is constantly bathed in stress hormones, key synapses, the connections between nerves, fail to form in critical regions of the brain. And the flood of stress chemicals doesn't just stop. It can go on for years and decades, biology gone haywire. At the simplest level, when the earliest experiences of the newborns are adequately stimulated, his or her neuronal connections grow, or neuronal pruning or stunting occurs.

The kind of emotional attunement provided by secure attachment actually increases blood flow to the prefrontal areas of the child's brain, resulting in the growth of neural tissue in the emotional and attentional centers of the brain. Without the emotional resonance provided by attunement from an attachment figure, the child's excitement and prefrontal arousal areas of the brain are dampened, and growth in regions of the brain that encourage inhibition is accelerated.

During critical times in development, if children have been pro-vided a poor attachment experience, their brains show less opiate receptor density, which makes it harder for them to regulate their affect and self-soothe.

"We can't persuade people with developmental trauma with a cognitive argument (cortex brain) or compel them with an emotional affect (limbic brain), if their brain stem (survival brain) is dysregulated," Perry warns. *"We can't talk people in this kind of alarm state into doing the right thing, because their thinking brain's been turned off by the alarm state. And we can't reach their emotional-attachment-relational (limbic) brain if they feel so threatened, they get into an alarm state, because they can't feel reward from relations with people.*[62]

Default mode network

When our brain is at rest, when nothing major is going on- when say, we are between intense feeling states – it is in a state of "idling," says Ruth Lanius, MD.[63] When the brain is idling, a network of neurocir-cuitry known as the brain's "default mode network" quietly hums along, like a car idling in the driveway.

Areas of the brain in the default mode network include those asso-ciated with memory, those that help us construct thought, to recognize that others have thoughts, and to help us as we integrate our thoughts. All those regions are integral to our internal thought process.

This network is always on standby, ready to help us figure out what we need to do next. "The dense connectivity in these areas of the brain helps us determine what's relevant or not relevant, so that we can be ready for whatever our environment is going to ask of us, " says Lanius. "It is also integrally connected to areas of the brain that relate one's sense of self, one's feeling state."[64]

People who have suffered trauma have very little connectivity in the default mode network. Their basic sense of self--who they are at the core, when at rest or at peace, is very weak. The brain seems not to have a healthy idling position, or to put it another way, equilibrium. Unpredictable chronic stressors of adverse childhood experience can hurt the neuroconnectivity in this part of the brain.

"Emotions become futile," says Lanius, "It would drive you crazy to be feeling a lot of emotions and yet to know you can't know what you feel, and so you become disassociated from your feeling state. You become emotionally unaware of what's going on around you." You downregulate your anxiety.[65]

Years later, this freezing or shutting off has immense consequences to adult relationships. We may simply turn off unpleasant feelings, unable to respond with compassion for ourselves or others, or be turned off by anyone showing signs of neediness in general.

Chapter Four

4.1 Defining Addiction

I felt it was important to include a brief discussion of addiction as a disease because I understand that the medical model is not universally accepted. It is an admission of my bias due to my long-term observation of the impact of addiction as its own process – not a symptom of another mental illness. This is true knowing that I have retained my own long-term recovery through a Twelve Step process, a spiritual program, which at times can seem confusing! The explanation I have come to for myself is that my long-term immersion in the Twelve Step process shored up my frontal lobe with guidance and wisdom and calmed my limbic system enough to learn to choose people instead of alcohol. It is also true that like many in recovery, I have received outside help to treat my ADHD/depression and childhood issues. It has taken a team to get me where I am! Due to needing a team, I am especially fond of the ASAM, American Society of Addiction Medicine, assessment which I will discuss in detail later. It considers six different areas of a person's life to create a treatment plan to treat addiction. Substance use disorder is multi-faceted and a complicated challenge!

Many treatment centers have adopted the American Society of Addiction Medicine (ASAM) definition and assessment of addiction, which includes the DSM 5 criteria for Substance Use Disorder. I recommend the ASAM diagnosis and DSM5 criteria as a suggested psychoeducational handout for use with residents because I believe it is imperative for them to have the opportunity to review the "official" criteria for addiction to better assess their own disease process. I often use the DSM 5 with residents when they are unsure about addiction. I grab the criteria and say, *"Would you like to know how counselors decide if someone is struggling with addiction?"* Acknowledging that I do not know how many of the criteria are true of them, I open to the criteria and read them through while asking the resident to tell me which ones apply. Using the criteria in this way allows an objective conversation rather than being perceived as lapsing into "accusation." Part of the surrender process in recovery is the client's opportunity to self-identify as an addict or alcoholic. As a side note, I am referring to surrender, often a triggering word for recovering folks, as the process where you stop trying to control your drinking so you can direct your energy to managing everything in your life.

Short Version of 2013 ASAM Definition[66]

Addiction is a primary, chronic disease of brain reward, motivation, memory, and related circuitry. Dysfunction in these circuits leads to characteristic biological, psychological, social and spiritual manifestations. This is reflected in an individual pathology pursuing reward and/ or relief by substance use and other behaviors.

Addiction is characterized by inability to consistently abstain, impairment in behavioral control, craving, diminished recognition of significant problems with one's behaviors and interpersonal relationships, and a dysfunctional emotional response. Like other chronic diseases, addiction often involves cycles of relapse and remission. Without treatment or engagement in recovery activities, addiction is progressive and can result in disability or premature death.

The 2019 ASAM Definition update:

Addiction is a treatable, chronic medical disease involving complex interactions among brain circuits, genetics, the environment, and an individual's life experiences. People with addiction use substances or engage in behaviors that become compulsive and often continue despite harmful consequences.

Prevention efforts and treatment approaches for addiction are generally as successful as those for other chronic diseases.

DSM 5[67] Substance Use Disorder spans a wide variety of problems arising from: substance use, and cover 11 different criteria:

- Taking the substance in larger amounts or for longer than you meant to
- Wanting to cut down or stop using the substance but not managing to
- Spending a lot of time getting, using, or recovering from use of the substance
- Cravings and urges to use the substance
- Not managing to do what you should at work, home or school, because of substance use
- Continuing to use, even when it causes problems in relationships

- Giving up important social, occupational or recreational activities because of substance use

- Using substances again and again, even when it puts you in danger

- Continuing to use, even when you know you have a physical or psychological problem that could have been caused or made worse by the substance

- Needing more of the substance to get the effect you want (tolerance)

- Development of withdrawal symptoms, which can be relieved by taking more of the substance.

The DSM 5 allows clinicians to specify how severe the substance use disorder is, depending on how many symptoms are identified. Two or three symptoms indicate a mild substance use disorder, four or five symptoms indicate a moderate substance use disorder, and six or more symptoms indicate a severe substance use disorder. Clinicians can also add "in early remission," "in sustained remission," "on maintenance therapy," and "in a controlled environment."

There are also colloquial definitions like, "Fun, fun with problems, problems." It is not true that someone needs to adopt an identity as an alcoholic or addict to enter recovery. We will discuss stages of change later. It is primarily important that we begin to help people learn to see that what started out as a solution to life's problems has BECOME the problem. When their use is addressed, life's problems become more manageable.

4.2 Neurobiology of Addiction

Both the ASAM and DSM5 sections lend themselves to a group format. Early attachment disruption interrupts the resident's ability to accurately self-reflect having not been accurately seen and heard as a child. As a result, their ability to "see" themselves contributes to an inability to connect the dots between situations in their life and their behavior. Providing residents with an understanding of addiction as altered neurology provides an opening for them to consider their behavior more objectively. Group counseling is particularly helpful here as the opportunity for recognition and identification can assist their struggling self-reflection skills.

The bottom line is that alcohol and drugs "hijack" the reward pathway in the limbic system and flood the system with the neurotransmitter dopamine. Ultimately, regardless of drug or choice, we are addicted to dopamine.

There are people in treatment, especially the avoidantly attached people, who will want to do a deep dive into the neurology of addiction, and you can provide them with information about the Reward Pathway. I also have referred them to *This Naked Mind: Control Alcohol, Find Freedom, Discover Happiness, and Change Your Life* by Annie Grace.

4.3 Brain Systems in Addiction and Attachment

Remember that we covered earlier that insecure attachment can lead to a dopamine deficiency, but there are other impacts as well. There are three dominant brain systems in addiction that have intriguing connections with attachment:

The Opioid Attachment-Reward System:

According to the brain opioid theory of social attachment, opioids may underlie the contented feelings associated with social connection and may be critical to continued bonding. Happy, attuned emotional interactions with parents stimulate a release of natural opioids in an infant's brain. This endorphin surge promotes the attachment relationship and the further development of the child's opioid and dopamine circuitry. In contrast, stress reduces the numbers of both opiate and dopamine receptors. Healthy growth of these crucial systems—responsible for such essential drives as love, connection, pain relief, pleasure, incentive and motivation—depends, therefore, on the quality of the attachment relationship. In addition, the opioid system controls pain, reward and addictive behaviors.

The endogenous opiate system in humans has been related to pain and placebo effect and recently, to social rejection and acceptance. Thus, some authors[68] talk about "social pain." Interestingly, the endogenous opiate system has a role in harm avoidance and in the reward system. These traits of personality (harm avoidance and reward dependence) predispose addicts to addictive disorders, and likely, pathological models of social bonding may drive to a need of relieving excessive discomfort created by opioid function altered through addictive behaviors. The origin of addictive disorder must be focused on the individual vulnerability rather than in the addictive substance/behavior.

In his text, *In the Realm of Hungry Ghosts: Close Encounters with Addiction,* [69] Gabor Mate includes the following quote from an addict,

"The first time I did heroin," she said to me, *"it felt like a warm, soft hug."* In that phrase, she told her life story and summed up the psychological and chemical cravings of all substance dependent addicts.

This observation is also made by Andreas Schindler in his *Front: Psychiatry 2019* article[70], who notes in the results of his research that insecure attachment indicates different patterns of attachment in different groups of substance abusers, suggesting different developmental pathways. "Fearful–avoidant attachment was frequent in heroin addicts."

The Dopamine-Based Incentive-Motivation Apparatus:

Dopamine levels in a baby's brain fluctuate, depending on the presence or absence of the parent. A study in four-month-old monkeys showed that major alterations of dopamine and other neurotransmitter systems occurred after only six days of separation from their mothers. "Loss of an important attachment appears to lead to less of an important neurotransmitter in the brain. *In vivo* studies have demonstrated that social-emotional stimulation is necessary for the growth of the nerve endings that release dopamine and for the growth of receptors to which dopamine needs to bind in order to do its work. Adult rats and mice kept in long-term isolation have a reduced number of dopamine receptors in the midbrain incentive circuits and, notably, in the frontal areas implicated in addiction."[71]

The Self-Regulation Areas of the Prefrontal Cortex:

Parental nurturing determines the levels of other key brain chemicals, too—including serotonin, the mood messenger enhanced by antidepressants like Fluoxetin. Peer-reared monkeys, separated from their mothers, have lower lifelong levels of serotonin than monkeys brought up by their mothers. In adolescence these same monkeys are more aggressive and are far more likely to consume alcohol in excess. Similar effects are seen with other neurotransmitters that are essential in regulating mood and behavior, such as norepinephrine. Even slight imbalances in the availability of these chemicals are manifested in aberrant behaviors like fearfulness and hyperactivity and increase the individual's sensitivity to stressors for a lifetime. In turn, such acquired traits increase the risk of addiction.[72]

Counseling Alters Nervous System

The good news is that the counseling relationship can make an important difference in re-aligning the prefrontal and limbic systems towards better connectivity and emotional regulation. The clinician as a secure base is crucial as a powerful attachment experience alters a person's nervous system. This is sometimes referred to as **co-regulating**. Individuals in an attachment relationship are provided help in regulating their nervous system by unconsciously acquiring implicit (unspoken bodily sensations, muscle memory, and perceptions) knowledge about the rules that govern healthy interpersonal relationships as they experience a safe relationship with the counselor. I am highlighting **experience** here because frontal lobe logic and understanding will not, alone, shift the nervous system. As we covered earlier, our systems are being developed before we ever have language, so we have a felt reality underneath our thoughts. **We need to experience safety to even recognize what it is.**

Residents often seem puzzled and say they do not know what they are feeling, often because they confuse sensations like craving with emotions. Counselors can help by identifying and putting into words emotions, replicating the mentalizing (*the exploration of the inner, mental world of oneself and others*) aspects required in attachment formation. Using our mirror neurons, we can infer someone else's mind by facial expression, tone of voice and non-verbal communication. It includes the action imitation, face imitation and intention understanding that communicates we see and hear their internal world accurately. This may call for us to be the container and receiver for intense, previously inarticulate pain and rage. Staying still and not retreating allows our residents to feel understood and validated – normalized as fellow humans, which can reduce their profound alienation.

As I write this, I feel a need to note that this is one of the reasons it is so important for clinicians utilizing the AIAT® model to have addressed, or be in the process of addressing, their own nervous system reactivity. If not, it will be almost impossible to be the container you need to be because it will be overwhelming. I am reminded of a neurodivergent client I was treating for treatment-resistant depression (medications had not worked) who had a horrendous childhood experience of being misunderstood and frequently blamed for his difficulty reading social situations or being rejected. He is acutely shame-based. He is also highly avoidantly attached, which means he hides in his intellect, and so had a history of being painfully misunderstood by clinicians who overestimated his intellectual understanding and did not register his shame-based emotionality. By the time I agreed to see him, he was very angry at the psychology field, dismissive of clinicians, and frequently disparaging therapists. He chose me because after interviewing several therapists, I was the only one who was Twelve Step focused. He had been working a CODA and now Adult Child of Alcoholics program and wanted to read me his Fourth Step inventory because he did not trust anyone enough to get a sponsor.

The first several resentments were towards previous therapists, and it was hard to hear. In fact, over the months of our work together, he frequently was reactive to thinking I might be giving him advice when I made observations – set ups for him to fail - and they were gentle ones. It took months for him to attempt to give me the benefit of the doubt that MAYBE it was his reaction versus my intention. There were times when I left these sessions feeling tired, even a little dispirited. It absolutely got better over time, and his ability to manage his reactivity progressed. But it took months. **A more substantial recovery may take years. This is why aftercare is the most important part of addiction treatment planning, in my estimation.**

Chapter Five

5.1 Stress as a Result of Addiction Cycle

Our emotional responses reflect our memory of these experiences and because of this, emotion is looked upon as an important organizer of mental activity that shapes our priorities, beliefs, and convictions. The actions of chronic stress, the result of the addiction cycle, can worsen the addict's emotional processing, recognition and regulation deficits, and appear as a severe form of dysfunction in emotional awareness, social attachment, and interpersonal relating. Addicted individuals suffer because they cannot regulate their emotions, self-other relations, and self-care.

We might not recognize dangerous or unhealthy situations and interactions, which allows us to enter or stay in relationships that are chaotic or harmful because they seem familiar and safe.

We may veer, with little warning, from a state of feeling to a state of heightened feeling. We may give too much in a relationship or to needy friends and family, because we're emotionally unattuned to our interior cues that should tell us we need to draw stronger boundaries – then we may erupt in anger when we realize that we're giving more than we are receiving. When feelings are threatening or overwhelming, opiates can be seductive in their ability to powerfully contain intense, disorganizing, and dysphoric emotions, especially rage and agitation. High doses of alcohol can also help contain intense affect.

Brains can show that individuals who lack emotional awareness have lost interconnected neurocircuitry in critical areas. The more emotionally unaware these individuals are, the less activation they show not only in the default mode network but also in an area of the brain known as the "insula," a region involved in interoceptive awareness – *how aware we are of our bodily cues that tune us into what's happening to us at the moment.* If feelings are defensively restricted and cut-off, the releasing properties of sedative hypnotics can allow the experience and expression of warmth and closeness that they otherwise cannot allow.

Lanius[73] has also found that those who have a dampened sense of emotionality show less activity in an area of the cortex, which indicates that: they are not self-reflective, they are not aware of what they feel emotionally, nor are they able to reflect on it mindfully." In the absence of fear, worry, anticipatory shame, or alarm in the face of potential harm and danger, especially those associated with addiction, self-care becomes less likely. Khantzian has suggested *"what gets most damaged with a trauma history is survival instincts"* [69]

This lack of awareness of feelings, this lack of consciousness as to how you might be contributing to disharmony or friction in a relationship, presents a problem for partners and parents since the only way to regulate yourself is the ability to reflect on your internal cues and impact on others. Without awareness you cannot be conscious of your behavior, and without consciousness of your behavior, you don't know how to improve your interactions in your most meaningful life experiences.

MRI studies also show that trauma decreases activity in an area of the brain that affects our ability to regulate and modulate emotions. When we have difficulty regulating our emotions and rebounding from stress, we are more kindled into anger. We may overreact to what we perceive as rejection, or injustice or have a knee-jerk reaction to disagreements and discord. We may become hyper-aggressive, argumentative, defensive and angry.

"When our emotions are under-regulated," explains Lanius, "This decreases our ability to dampen down intense feelings leading to greater activity in the amygdala, which regulates our emotional reactivity."[75]

Some of us over-modulate. Feeling so anxious and unable to process our feelings that we get quiet, we double-down, passively retreat and avoid confrontation at all costs. We may feel overwhelmed by feelings of loss and betrayal.

It's important to be familiar with your specific stress response because we can respond with fight, flight, or freeze responses as we learned in the Polyvagal section. When planning interventions for us or the residents, we need to keep in mind:

(Fight) Overexcited stress response – If you tend to become angry, agitated, or keyed up under stress, you will respond best to stress relief activities that quiet you down.

(Flight) Under excited stress response – If you tend to become depressed, withdrawn, or spaced out under stress, you will respond best to stress relief activities that are stimulating and that energize your nervous system.

(Freeze) Frozen stress response (both overexcited and under excited) – If you tend to freeze—speeding up in some ways while slowing down in others—you tend to check out or leave your body. Your challenge is to identify stress relief activities that will allow you to feel safe to inhabit your body and feel centered.

Also keep in mind that excess stress does not always show up as the "feeling" of being stressed, especially if you down-regulate or leave your body. *Many stresses go directly into our physical body and may only be recognized by the physical symptoms we manifest.*

5.2 Biology is NOT Destiny

We can reboot our brains. We can regain muscle tone. We can recover function in interconnected areas of the brain. The brain and body are never static; they are always in the process of becoming and changing.

Even if we have been set on high reactive mode for decades or a lifetime, we can still dial it down. We can respond to life's inevitable stressors more appropriately and shift away from an over-reactive inflammatory response. We can become neurobiologically resilient. We can turn bad epigenetics into good epigenetics and rescue ourselves.

We can create new neurons, make new synaptic connections, promote new patterns of thoughts and reactions, bring under-connected areas of the brain back online, and reset our stress response so that we decrease the inflammation that makes us ill.

Several candidate mechanisms, including endogenous opioids, oxytocin, and dopamine, have also been proposed as links between interdependent attachment and decreased negative affect. For example, opioid tone, or basal levels of opioid activity, may play a role in limiting levels of stress reactivity in a variety of contexts ,[76] and opioid activity can increase in the presence of social resources. [77]

Section Two:
Treatment Application of the Attachment Infused Addiction Model® (AIAT)

Chapter One

Now that we have spent some time reviewing the underlying theoretical structure of the Attachment Infused Addiction Treatment® model, we are prepared to start to construct a clinical approach.

1.1 Treatment Team Composition

The Attachment Infused Addiction Treatment® model is a connection and relationship development centered model. The staffing composition needs to be chosen based on staff members' willingness to be educated and function as connection facilitators, which means they possess the ability to model and support emotional regulation and transparency. As trauma-informed communicators, the staff is able to implement relationship repair strategies, anticipating that residents will have impairments in their ability to develop, maintain, or sustain secure attachments. In this model, the staff includes everyone from the cook and van driver to the Clinical Supervisor.

Primary Counter-Transference Challenge

One of the biggest challenges to integration of substance use and mental health staffing is found in our very different approach to **control.**

As Stephanie Brown points out in her seminal work, *A Developmental Model of Alcoholism and Recovery*, "Alcoholism and other addictions are related to power. In its essence, addiction is characterized by a distorted, faulty belief in the power of self – the power to control one's use of a substance."[78]

In general, mental health workers have been trained to support clients to increase their capacity for personal **control.** We utilize theories and strategies all created to assist clients to increase their self-awareness, their autonomy, and ability to direct their own lives. As a result, we largely expect clients to willingly participate in treatment unless blocked by unconscious defenses versus overt lying. We are committed to self-actualization and an internal locus of control, relying largely on the clients to direct the process and goals of the therapeutic treatment. Mistaking attachment for unhealthy dependence, mental health clinicians may even be dismayed by deepening support group involvement and attachment fearful of a new "addiction." If addiction is a learned behavior or coping strategy only, perhaps a strategy the counselor themselves may be using, it can be unlearned and is subject to self-control. In fact, the counselor may have been raised in an alcoholic or drug using family and may have over-relied on personal "control" and will to manage the impact of the addiction. If addiction is a strategy, controlled or moderate drinking or drug use may be possible once the underlying psychological distress is addressed.

The heart of substance use counseling is to encourage the client to surrender their attempts to control their use of drugs and alcohol. They have lost control. Addiction counselors work with clients to **allow** external support and form new attachments to explore the disease of addiction, coping skills, and trigger management through a counselor or support group until recovery becomes internalized.

Commonly, substance use counselors are recovering addicts themselves and may have a strong vested interest in the recovery of clients who often remind them of themselves, both a strength and a potential counter-transference problem. Using active and even more directive approaches than in traditional mental health counseling, Motivational Interviewing and CBT are utilized to support client willingness to separate from the substance by examining the unmanageable consequences of using. This helps reframe the problems the client presents as the result of their chemical use versus character. Underlying emotional issues are potential triggers for relapse and addressed through that frame, believing that substance abuse treatment should be primary as using substances makes counseling ineffective. If addiction is the result of a physiological disease process, then remission through abstinence is the only realistic option.

In *A Place Called Self: Women, Sobriety, and Radical Transformation*, author Stephanie Brown describes the shift in control in our addiction:

"You start to build your sense of self on a false belief, the belief that you can control your drinking or other addictive behavior. This isn't an easy thing to do. Since you really don't have control, you're going to have to lie to yourself in order to believe you are not addicted. You have to tell yourself more and more elaborate lies over time, as evidence to the contrary becomes more and more compelling, and you have to rationalize or explain it away. All your energy goes into pretending...

... Our need to tell ourselves that we can control our addiction becomes the organizing principle for our lives; it dictates everything we say and every move we make. It's a heavy burden, and ultimately it becomes one of the heaviest burdens of all, the burden of emptiness. (pp 18-19).[79]

Keep in mind that denial is a protective defense strategy. Maryann Amodeo[80] points out that among the painful realizations and feelings may include: the shock of learning that one has a chronic, progressive, and potentially fatal illness; dread of the social stigma for oneself and family; fear of facing a life of abstinence with no dependable "escape hatch" for dealing with intolerable feelings or anxiety-provoking events; having to face traumatic memories, painful tosses, and past experiences without an anesthetic; guilt and shame about harming others during the drinking and drugging episodes; shame at having "done this to myself" and having not seen the problem sooner; grief over lost opportunities and relationships during the drinking and drugging career.

Impact of Early Trauma

The reality is the majority of residents participating in the Attachment Infused Addiction Treatment® Model will have significant scores on the CDC-Kaiser Permanente Adverse Childhood Experiences (ACE), and it is important to keep in mind that trauma impacts not only psychological well-being but has neurological impact. The most likely impact is a heightened sympathetic nervous response, *so they will be quick to interpret incoming data as threatening regardless of the communicator's intent.* Cognitive distortion is common when in a heightening fight, flight, or freeze reaction, with most likely interpretations and level of threat informed by their early attachment disruption management strategies. At the simplest level, some clients will move towards the threat and try to "force" resolution to the perceived attachment disruption. Some will retreat physically or emotionally to down-regulate their emotional state, and others will dissociate and freeze so no longer take in attempts to communicate or communicate incongruently. These strategies will at times trigger staff attachment history, so **staff will need to have a strong awareness of their own personal relationship triggers in order to utilize their emotional regulation skills in the moment.**

In addition to a heightened sympathetic nervous response to perceived threat created by a disruption in attachment with staff, a common trauma response is difficulty accessing language and disjointed sentence structure. The treatment team will need to be able to identify breakdowns in the resident's ability to communicate for neurological reasons, rather than define their inability as unwillingness or resistance.

While treatment staffing will include certified addiction counselors and master's level counselors, available access to psychiatric assessment and a more holistically trained medical professional will be vital to address the initial detoxification process and inevitable physical damage created by ongoing relational and life stressors as well as addiction. The use of peer counselors will be imperative. The peer counselors will be assigned to specific clients and will follow them for a year into their recovery, and relationship development with residents will begin from treatment admission.

Peer Recovery Support

Peer recovery support is a peer-based mentoring, education, and support service provided by individuals in recovery from substance use disorders to individuals with substance use disorders or co-occurring substance use and mental disorders. Use of peers in treatment is now commonly accepted as part of the continuum of services to promote recovery from substance use disorders. Peer providers often identify and help identify resources that residents may need to restructure their lives and further develop life skills. This may include acting as a liaison with formal treatment services or social services or assisting with referrals or linkages to medical care, employment support, human services, and other systems of care. More broadly, peer providers serve as advocates for the individual and the recovery community, conduct outreach, and act as role models.

Dr. David Best [81] has offered extensive research into the development of recovery capital – or what Cloud & Grandfield [82] define recovery capital as "the breadth and depth of internal and external resources that can be drawn upon to initiate and sustain recovery from AOD [alcohol and other drug] problems". Dr. Best has pioneered the Rec-Cap Training Model [83] to promote ongoing recovery and social connectedness, a collaboration tool between resident and peer counselor, that provides a roadmap to monitor resident progress from a strength-based and asset development perspective. Dr. Best identifies monitors asset-based community domains to include mutual aid groups (MA), recreation and sport (R&S), volunteering, education and employment (VEE), peer and recovery community groups (PRCG). The key to understanding his work is to recognize how much it is centered in the direct and personal connections facilitated by the peer to community assets beyond the treatment center. The development of healthy attachments between the consumer and the peer provider may mediate emotional regulation.

1.2 The Role of Psychoeducation

Psychoeducation originally developed working with psychiatric patients and has been adapted to working with addicts and alcoholics. The Attachment Infused Addiction Treatment® model makes a deliberate attempt to strengthen the neuronal connections between the executive functions and the limbic system for stronger emotional regulation. Learning is an effective way to stimulate neuronal growth.

Important elements in psychoeducation include:

- Information transfer (symptomatology of the disturbance, causes, treatment concepts, etc.)
- Emotional discharge (understanding to promote exchange of experiences with others.)
- Support of a medication or psychotherapeutic treatment as co-operation is promoted between the mental health and chemical dependency professional and client (compliance, adherence).
- Assistance to self-help (e.g. training, as crisis situations are promptly recognized and what steps should be taken to be able to help the client).

Facilitation encourages much more exchange of information, which was coined by American educator Malcom Knowles as "learner-centered" education.[84] Knowles believed adults would learn better if they were more involved in the decisions about their own learning, and we can summarize his model on six assumptions:

- Adults have a "need to know." They must have a rationale for why they need to learn a body of content.
- Adults come to the educational setting with more relevant experience.
- Adults have a need to be involved in the decisions about their own learning.

- Adults learn best when they see a direct **relevance** of information to their own lives.

- Adults are better at learning content that is oriented towards solving problems.

- Adults respond better to intrinsic motivation rather than extrinsic motivation.

The Attachment Infused Addiction Treatment® model was created for an extended treatment episode to allow a detox and stabilization phase while the initial attachment with the treatment facility staff is developing. Each resident is ideally matched with a peer counselor who will follow the resident over the next year. The ideal AIAT® resident has attempted addiction treatment previously and relapsed and may or may not have a co-occurring disorder. It is quite likely that they will have experienced two or more of the ACE indicators contributing to their early attachment disruption. When residents first arrive, they will most likely be in physical and emotional distress, and medical evaluation and kind hospitality to support the expectedly elevated hyper or hypo arousal state will be a priority. From an attachment-based view, this is key time of client vulnerability for staff to position themselves as accurate and timely responders to resident needs, which has most likely not been their experience when in earlier distress. *This is a corrective experience opportunity from the outset and should not be overlooked or undervalued.*

Chapter Two

2.1 Phase One

By the time Phase One has ended, residents will have taken the ACE and the Readiness Ruler. They will have been introduced to the basics of attachment strategies, constructed a Sensory Tool Box, and identified key emotional regulation strategies they will be using throughout their stay. They will have identified and stabilized their withdrawal, cravings, and begin strengthening their immune system.

As we begin this section, I want to refer back to out earlier theoretical discussion to remind us that the presence of consistent caregiver contact in infancy is one factor in the normal development of the brain's neurotransmitter systems; the absence of it makes the child more vulnerable to "needing" drugs of abuse later in life to supplement what their brain is lacking. Another key factor is the *quality* of the contact the caregiver provides, which in large part, is dependent on the caregiver's mood and stress level.

Let's refer back to our earlier theory, *The caregivers' acceptance of the child's emotions as well as their ability and willingness to openly communicate about them,* **encourages emotional awareness and self-regulation** *in the child. . . Clinicians like Mary Ainsworth point out the parent's ability to accept protest without retaliation or excessive anxiety is also a key determinant of secure attachment. The child must be welcomed back with unconditional intimacy."*[85]

As we enter the counseling relationship, we have an immediate opportunity for residents to experience the importance of their internal states as we reflect back to them our curiosity and genuine interest in their physical state, emotions and thoughts. This attachment stance coordinates well with empathy and collaboration-infused Motivational Interviewing strategies. Maintaining consistent attachment requires us to be aware that some of these states will be reactive and defensive, and our attachment position is to remain steady and avoid rejection in the face of client attempts to distance or lapse into neediness if triggered by an unconscious desire to trust us. We need to be continually mindful that trusting an attachment to a person or group is risky for the resident, because to trust and then lose the abandonment is a replication of the childhood wound that led to the addiction we are treating!

The characteristics of a secure attachment outlined by John Bowlby provide us with behavioral observation points to determine if we are making progress with our attempts to engage the resident's willingness to attach in these first weeks:

Safe Haven: When the resident feels threatened or afraid, he or she can return to the counseling staff for comfort and soothing.

Secure Base: The counseling staff provides a secure and dependable base for the resident to take emotional and behavioral risks in the pursuit of long-term recovery.

Proximity Maintenance: The resident strives to stay near the counseling staff and program to assist them with emotional and physical stability when in distress.

Separation Distress: When considering premature program completion or counselor absence, the resident will feel uneasy, anxious, and may protest.

2.2 Trauma Informed Settings

Residents are most likely to sustain their attachment efforts in a trauma-informed setting. According to SAMHSA's concept of a trauma-informed approach[86], "A program, organization, or system that is trauma-informed:

Realizes the widespread impact of trauma and understands potential paths for recovery;

Recognizes the signs and symptoms of trauma in clients, families, staff, and others involved with the system;

Responds by fully integrating knowledge about trauma into policies, procedures, and practices; and Seeks to actively resist *re-traumatization*."

At its best, trauma-informed care (TIC) is resilience-informed care. It's an overall approach, at the individual, organizational, and systemic levels that uses respect and consideration of trauma histories to create safety and hope for clients. Truly effective TIC recognizes human vulnerability, but still insists on finding and mobilizing survivors' strengths, resources, and capacity for healing and recovery.

In these early days, we are engaging the resident through genuine attention to their neurological and emotional state. The specific goal for hyperactivated patients is to reduce their need for reassurance from others and "talk themselves off the cliff"; and for the deactivated patient, the goal is to reduce their tendency to cut off emotional experience.

2.3 How do we accomplish this?

Wallin,[87] says that secure base is promoted by collaborative communication, which involves four elements:

2.3a Fostering a collaborative dialogue that is inclusive of all domains of experience.

We actively demonstrate interest and support for the internal and external experience of the clients. How well can they identify their emotions, their physical responses, their arousal levels? What role in their life does the substance play and how do they feel they have been impacted by their addiction? What do they believe contributes to where they are at this moment?

Khantznian[88] emphasizes that forming an effective therapeutic alliance requires a shift from a typical one in which the patient can feel scolded about what the drugs are doing to them, to one where an understanding is offered as to what the drug is doing for them. This counters the harsh shame of drug use experienced in relational settings which has become internalized.

Keep in mind that all behaviors are purposeful, including the use of substances:

- Self-medicating intrusive voices
- Avoiding loneliness
- Escaping a terrible reality
- Enhancing a boring an empty existence
- Avoiding horrible withdrawal symptoms
- Maintaining substance–based friendships and relationships

The question is always, "What does the drug do for you?"

Our empathy point is that addiction is a tragic consequence to a behavior that began for a beneficial reason or a purpose. We are empathetic to the client's view of the benefits of their behavior to manage their unbearable pain. This is not an acceptance, approval, or affirmation of their behaviors; it is merely empathy to the resident's view that their drug and or alcohol use is, at this time in their lives, seen as helpful. "I understand your view that alcohol helps manage your grief. Would you like to spend some time with me while we talk about some other ways you can learn to manage this pain?"

2.3b Actively identifying ongoing ruptures and fostering repair

When working with a resident with a clear history of relational and emotional abandonment, it is to be expected that human imperfection of the counselor will ultimately slam into the expectations of the attachment-disrupted resident. While this contrast might be experienced as painful to the anxious and disorganized attached client reacting to their idealization of the counselor, the avoidantly attached client will simply downregulate and feel comforted by their ability to predict the disappointment that has been their life experience.

This apparent therapeutic "rupture" will no doubt stimulate a resident's early childhood attachment strategies, which can range from anxious clinging and tantruming to force greater attachment to harsh detachments and dismissiveness to remain disconnected. *This is a vulnerable place for the attachment-disrupted clinician*, who will likely be triggered by the same strategies they may have encountered with their attachment disrupted parents in their own childhoods. In this case, our instinct will be to label the resident with a psychological label such as "personality disorder," "borderline," "con artist," attention seeking" to maintain our own emotional safety in their presence. **While all of these long-term well-honed strategies for survival could certainly be true, they are strategies, not character.**

Treatment Staff Need to Monitor Their Emotional Regulation in the Face of Attachment Disruption

Our immediate task when triggered is to utilize the tools we have learned to lower our personal arousal states. This allows us to retain the available and responsive attachment stance that will be vital to the success of the resident to develop emotional regulation skills. When triggered, it may help to default to your frontal lobe and review the ACES study that is the evidence for the importance of trauma-informed treatment settings.

After WE are feeling stabilized, we can initiate the following corrective experience. These steps will be necessary throughout the treatment episode. We are required to initiate a conversation about the behavioral strategies we are seeing and invite the resident to tell us in full detail what they are thinking and feeling ABOUT US with a clear verbal and nonverbal commitment to stay connected to them. Our empathetic connection to them is unconditional.

1. We need to validate their perspective, and gently offer to share our internal experience of the same incident and the impact of their behavior ON US. We see them and they matter enough to impact us. This demonstrates emotional regulation skills and willingness to be the emotional container of what will be a hard level of intimacy for them.

2. Solicit from the client what will be necessary to repair the rupture and move forward.

2.3c Application Example

Carlos has become increasingly agitated in the group and Sandy is sharing her experience of feeling bullied by him earlier during chore completion. As the counselor is supporting her to share her feelings using "I statements" and not blaming, Carlos suddenly stands up and yells at the counselor, *"You always do this. It's ALWAYS me!"* and storms out of the group to the back area to get a cigarette. This catches the counselor by surprise as he has been focusing on coaching Sandy, and he finds himself facing the remaining clients who are waiting to see what he will do.

The counselor, Robert, decides to be transparent with the group.

"Well, I didn't see that coming. Carlos was obviously feeling attacked. Is that what you saw?"

(By giving the group a chance to share their observations and experiences, Robert can validate that they may have been triggered themselves when this interruption took place. As each member shares, Robert is able to hear them and even share HIS experience with them. **He is demonstrating a clear verbal and nonverbal desire to remain connected to the group.** Once Robert has sufficiently addressed the impact on the group, he can continue with the natural flow of the group.)

After group, Robert finds Carlos out in the smoking area and attempts to address what happened earlier.

"Hi, Carlos. I'm sorry you felt you had to leave the group so abruptly. You seemed to feel like I was attacking you in some way, is that right?"

"It's always my fault."

"What's always your fault?"

"Whenever shit goes wrong here, it's always somehow about me!"

"What have I said or done to make you think that I am always blaming you? I know that is not my intention, so I genuinely want to know what you are seeing and hearing when I'm with you?"

This question is key here because it indicates to Carlos that the counselor is open to feedback and is genuinely interested in maintaining a connection to Carlos even after Carols has pushed him away. If the counselor can remain non-defensive, Carlos may be able to settle his reactivity enough to begin to look at his own behavior and see that it might be affecting other people. He also might have the chance to see the situation from the counselor's perspective, increasing his ability to "mentalize."

2.3d Upgrading the dialogue and the mentalizing to "higher levels of awareness"

Fonagy and colleagues,[89] found a strong relationship between attachment styles and a person's capacity to think about oneself in relation to others. They called this ability the reflexive self-function (RSF) which reflects a person's capacity for inner speech and insight. The acquiring of inner speech means a person can be intimate with oneself, which goes hand in hand with the development of empathy and knowledge of self. The hallmark of the securely attached individual is the ability to talk about his or her attachment history in a coherent, succinct manner without becoming lost in the narrative, altering the story to preserve a desired impression, or discounting emotionally salient events.

Mentalization in counseling, much like the infant-parent dynamic, is a process of joint awareness in which the patient's mental states are the object of attention. Optimally, patient and counselor are engaged in a process of eliciting implicit unidentified and nonverbal information to hopefully make the information explicit and available to assist them in their recovery.[91] **From an attachment perspective we are helping the resident to "hear themselves" in the presence of a non-judgmental listener.**

Authors Daniel P. Brown and David S. Elliott in *Attachment Disturbances in Adults*[92] offer helpful Tips for Therapist on Influencing Mentalizing, including: maintaining an inquisitive, curious, not-knowing stance, offering interventions that are simple and to the point; maintaining a balance between engaging patient exploring mental states of self and others; engaging in a mirroring process in which your emotional responsiveness reflects the patient's mental state and feelings back to the patient; letting the resident know what you are thinking of as to permit the resident to correct your distorted mentalizing; and acknowledging mistakes and actively exploring your contribution to the resident's adverse reactions.

The rules that determine how to relate are difficult to unlearn because this information is not available to explicit, fact based, memory. Flores[87], points out that direct experience, and not insightful explanations, are influential in altering or modifying this type of memory. As Lewis said, *"Insight is the popcorn of therapy.* [88] Real change requires direct experience.

We will discuss the assessment and development of reflexive self-function skills in the later stages of the treatment. In this early phase, the focus will be on assisting the newly recovering resident to consider the vantage point of others, including the counselor, in addition to assisting them to consider their own internal reality.

Let's return to our **Application Example**

Carlos responds to Robert, *"It's like you were letting Sandy call me out in front of the group. That's not how you "do" people, know you? You guys here do that kind of thing all the time!"*

"So, when I was helping Sandy tell you how she was feeling, it felt like I was putting you on blast?"

"Exactly! Why do you do that?"

"Well, one of the reasons people use drugs is because they don't know how to talk about what they're feeling. So, instead of expressing themselves, they just get loaded. Can you relate to that?"

"Yeah," Carlos says cautiously.

"Sandy had a feeling about the way you talked to her during chores, and I saw it as a good chance for her to practice."

"So, it's okay to call me out just so SHE can learn something?"

"I can see now why you see it like that, though I thought it was a chance for you to learn something also."

"Like what?"

"Like the fact that what you say to other people matters. That you affect people, and you matter. I also hoped you would feel closer to her afterwards."

"Then why didn't you SAY so instead of just coming at me?"

"You're right, I knew what I was thinking, but I didn't say it out loud." Robert concedes. *"It would have been better to tell you what was in my head instead of just doing it."*

2.3e Providing a real relationship to which therapists and patient alike struggle with and fully engage with each other. We provide a corrective experience.

Just as reflexive self-reflection can only develop in an attachment relationship where the child does not have to be preoccupied with the availability or well-being of the mother, the insecurely attached resident who does not have to be preoccupied with threats to the counselor attachment is more likely to be oneself in their presence. A clinician's openness regarding their thinking about the assessment and treatment plan establishes the cooperative system and is the foundation of treatment collaboration from the outset.

The importance of kindness, empathy, respectful support cannot be overstated as we attempt to provide effective attunement to their needs to be seen and heard accurately and can validate how their relational distrust and addictive disease leave them so susceptible to attachment to addictive substances. Substance using clients respond more favorably to a counselor who is direct, spontaneous, and engaging than the more traditional observing counselor. *Available and engaging counselors can counter the chronic feelings of boredom, deadness, meaninglessness, and inner emptiness that threatens to overtake them.* [93]

Final return to Application Example

Carlos is surprised that Robert is telling him what he was thinking, and even more surprised Robert admits he might be wrong.

"I get it man. You were just doing your job. I shouldn't have flipped out like that."

"I appreciate that, Carlos. I can see where I need to work more on what I keep telling you guys, which is letting people into our thinking!" Robert says with a laugh. *"Carlos, Can I ask you something else?'*

"Sure"

"It feels like this feeling blamed thing is not new – like you have felt this way before. Am I right?"

"Well, I was always the problem as a kid, if that's what you mean."

"That's exactly what I mean. I wonder if because you got blamed a lot as a kid you might sometimes think people are blaming you even when they aren't? What do you think?"

"Like it's what you call a "trigger?"

"Yeah. When you get triggered, what happens in your body?"

Carlos thinks for a minute. *"I feel hot inside, and I feel like I need to move."*

"Do you feel like you need to move toward what's bothering you or away from it?"

"I feel like getting away from it."

"Like in group. Did you feel hot before you left group?"

"Yeah, I did."

"I'm going to ask you to do an experiment with me if you're willing."

"Like what?" Carlos asks hesitantly.

"The next time you feel hot like that, and I am there, I want you to try telling me what's happening in your body. I want to see if we can figure out how you can calm down without having to run."

"So, you want me to stay trapped?"

"No, you can leave if it doesn't work. But I want to try and give you a new tool to be able to CHOOSE when you leave or stay. Right now, you're triggered, and you don't control your movements. I'd like to try and help you have more choices."

"Oh, that's cool," Carlos agrees.

Chapter Three

3.1 Early Assessment and Psychoeducation: Integration of Motivation Interviewing with Attachment Theory

The road to recovery requires careful balance between affect release and affect containment.[94]

Theorists Flores, Wright, and Khantznian[95] discuss the attachment implications in the treatment of addictions, stating that it begins with abstinence and detachment from the object of addiction which is the client's drug of choice. To accomplish establishing a baseline for a resident's willingness to enter abstinence to allow the attachment-based strategies to be implemented further, both mental health and substance abuse counselors will begin with Motivational Interviewing (MI) to create the therapeutic alliance.

"Intrinsic motivation for change occurs in an accepting, empathetic relationship in which the person discovers that current behaviors keep them from achieving what is wanted and valued in their lives."[96]

Motivational Interviewing is a foundational approach to effective substance abuse counseling, and because Motivational Interviewing is transtheoretical, it provides a logical theory to integrate with Attachment Theory. In fact, an attachment-infused use of MI fully fits the spirit of Motivational Interviewing as conceived by founder William Miller as the spirit of partnership, acceptance, evocation and compassion are also an integral part of attachment formation.

Collaboration (Partnership): "We are going to work together."

Autonomy (Acceptance): "I value you and am delighted to talk with you."

Evocation: "I am going to create a space for you to share yourself and your story with me."

Compassion: "I want to understand and respect you and your experience."

In particular, acceptance in the context of motivational interviewing includes affirmation and is really about is reinforcing those specific things the client says or does that may assist in understanding and/or making a change. Additionally, accurate empathy is a core skill of MI and is the ability to accurately convey to the client that you are really trying to understand what's going on with them and what this problem means to them.

Evocation means to draw out of the client their own perceptions, goals and values, thus the counseling relationship starts with the assumption that the resources and motivation for change reside in the client. In practice, this means that the counselor is eliciting from the client, rather than imparting information or opinions and so is doing more listening than talking. Translating the mentalization of early attachment into psychotherapy into developing *metacognitive (reflecting on one's thoughts and thoughts of others) skill* is a process of joint awareness in which the client's mental states are the object of attention.

There are three ways to develop metacognitive skills: **validation, therapist self-disclosure pertaining to mental states, and therapist sharing of experiences pertaining to mental states.**[93] Counselors high in evocation are curious and patient. They give the resident the benefit of the doubt about wanting to change and show a focused intent to draw out the resident's own desire and reasons for changing by demonstrating consistent interest in their internal world.

3.2 Assessment Strategies

In Phase One we are spending time with residents, gathering formal and informal assessment information, introducing emotional regulation techniques, and psychoeducation for foundational understanding. The American Society of Addiction Medicine (ASAM) assessment is a widely used instrument for gathering multiple dimensions of data for optimal treatment and discharge planning. It coordinates well with the Prochaska and DiClemente Stages of Change to establish the starting place for level of care and dosage of intervention.

3.2a Physical/Emotional Evaluation and Stabilization

In the population for the Attachment Infused Addiction Treatment® model, the appropriate level would be an extended stay in residential treatment with a history of treatment failure, so *a diagnosed co-occurring disorder will be a high probability.*

Residents need to be educated that in addition to the symptoms of their depression, PTSD, or anxiety, they will soon be struggle with:

- Cravings for their drug of choice

- A tolerance to their drug of choice, requiring higher and higher doses

- Increased episodes of mental health symptoms

- More intensive or longer-lasting mental health symptoms

- Experience of withdrawal symptoms and Post-Acute Withdrawal Syndrome (PAWS)

It will be essential that residents receive integrated treatment, which includes simultaneous psychiatric and addiction treatment, and a co-occurring focused psychoeducation group would be helpful here. It is helpful to assess the resident using the AIAT® Life Areas Rating Scale, which allows the resident to consider the connection between substance use and mental health.

AIAT® Life areas assessment rating

How much are each of these areas a problem for you? Rate 0 – 5

0 = no problem, 1 = little problem, 2 = minor problem, 3 = somewhat of a problem, 4 = major problem, 5 = overwhelming problem H

How much alcohol or drug use contributes: Rate on 0-5 scale,

0 = no contribution, 1 = a little contribution, 2 = somewhat contributes, 3 = fair contribution, 4 = mostly contributes, 5 = completely contributes

How much psychiatric problems contribute

0 = no contribution, 1 = a little contribution, 2 = somewhat contributes, 3 = fair contribution, 4 = mostly contributes, 5 = completely contributes

Life area	How much of a	Substance Related	Mental Health Con-	Comments
Family relationships				
Spouse/partner				
Parenting				
Work				
Financial				
Physical Well-Being				
Emotional Well-				
Friendships				
Self-Esteem				
Spirituality				
Other (specify)				

Change Plan Worksheet

My current problem that I would like to address is:
The changes I would like to make related to this are:
The most important reasons why I want to make these changes are:

Given the impact of chronic stress on their immune system, it is quite possible that there will be any range of systemic illness to be addressed in addition to the lower bone density and nutritional deficiencies that normally accompany residents in addiction treatment. These could include adrenal system depletion, high blood pressure, arrhythmia, chronic pain, fibromyalgia, and diabetes.

In addition, diminished dopamine levels because of ongoing substance abuse may create depression and anxiety that may be severe enough to require psychiatric medication for stabilization. In addition, the emergence of PTSD and other significant symptoms of early trauma and neglect may also require immediate psychiatric assessment and treatment.

Treatment for deficiencies needs to be initiated immediately through a combination of allopathic, naturopathic, behavioral and dietary interventions.[97] This may include the introduction to medically assisted treatment like Campral or Vivitrol for craving management. It may also include the reintroduction of psychiatric medication which has been reviewed for efficacy and dosage once the addictive substances have been removed or reduced.

3.2b American Society of Addiction Medicine (ASAM)

Within Phase One, it will be important for the primary counselor to administer the American Society of Addiction Medicine (ASAM) assessment that provides an overview of the resident's drug and mental health history, which includes the DSM 5 criteria for Substance Use Disorder. It is my experience that the majority of substance abuse residents I have treated have never seen the criteria for substance use disorder, and I routinely share with them the DSM 5 criteria and collaboratively complete the assessment. It can be eye-opening to them to see what the professionals have used when evaluating them. You could also use assessments tools like the MAST or AUDIT. ASAM printable assessments are available online.

Assessment of Biopsychosocial Severity and Function in the common language of six ASAM Criteria dimensions determine needs and strengths.

ASSESSMENT DIMENSIONS	ASSESSMENT AND TREATMENT PLANNING FOCUS
1. Acute intoxication and/or withdrawal potential	Assessment for intoxication or withdrawal management. Withdrawal management in a variety of levels of care and preparation for continued addiction services
2. Biomedical conditions and complications	Assess and treat co-occurring physical health conditions or complications. Treatment provided within the level of care or through coordination of physical health services
3. Emotional, behavioral, or cognitive conditions and complications	Assess and treat co-occurring diagnostic or subdiagnostic mental health conditions or complications. Treatment provided within the level of care or through coordination of mental health services
4. Readiness to change	Assess stage of readiness to change. If not ready to commit to full recovery, engage into treatment using motivational enhancement strategies. If ready for recovery, consolidate and expand action for change.
5. Relapse, continued use, or continued problem potential	Assess readiness for relapse prevention services and teach where appropriate. Identify previous periods of sobriety or wellness and what worked to achieve this. If still at early stages of change, focus on raising consciousness of consequences of continued use or continued problems as part of motivational enhancement strategies.
6. Recovery environment	Assess need for specific individualized family or significant others, housing, financial, vocational, educational, legal, transportation, child care services. Identify any supports and assets in any or all of the areas.

I will be exploring the ASAM in more detail as we move forward. When we begin to explore the Outpatient application of the AIAT® Model, there will be specific ASAM criteria illustrated.

Psychoeducation:

In Phase One, it will be helpful for residents to have attended psychoeducation groups on the neurobiology of addiction, including the reward system, to help them connect to the neurological impact of trauma they will consider in the later phases of the treatment episode.

It will be helpful to administer the ACE Questionnaire and introduce basic psychoeducation information about the immune system and its impact of early attachment disruption often created by adverse events in a young person's life.

3.2c The ACE Study

One of the more convincing and powerful studies, The CDC-Kaiser Permanente Adverse Childhood Experiences (ACE) Study, is one of the largest investigations of childhood abuse and neglect and later-life health and well-being.[98] The ACE study shows a clear scientific link between many types of childhood adversity and adult onset of physical diseases and mental health disorders. The key is that the stressors are UNPREDICTABLE. When exploring the ACE Study with clients, it will be important to introduce what Mark Seery calls The Upside of Adversity[95] to balance the likely results of their scores.

Upside of Adversity

Mark Seery, PhD, has been searching for the upside of adversity, asking whether some stress exposure might make people stronger over the long term. Seery had hundreds of patients who suffered from chronic, debilitating back pain complete a survey about their lifetime exposure to 37 different types of stressful experiences.

Patients who had experienced absolutely no prior adversity in their childhood fared just as poorly as those who had experienced high levels of adversity," he says.[99] In other words, those participants who had a score of 0 on all childhood adversity questions – including the mild stressors Seery had included – were just as likely to be deeply disabled by their back pain and seek treatment for anxiety and depression as were those who had experienced significant levels of adversity when they were young.

On the other hand, patients who had met up with some adversity when they were young, but not too much, were least likely to be disabled due to back pain later in life, or to seek later treatment for anxiety or depression. Experiencing the right dose of hardship as a child or teenager helped build coping skills, resilience, and perspective to meet the challenge of dealing with debilitating, chronic pain in one's adult life. Having faced moderate stress in the past seemed to help individuals cope with newly occurring stressors happening in the here and now, says Seery. "They seemed to have gained a sense that when bad things happen that doesn't mean it's always going to be that bad.[100]

"We're not talking about the need to eliminate stress," he explains. "In children's lives, learning to deal with normative stress is part of healthy development." Normative stress helps kids learn to seek out resourceful strategies, self-soothe, recover, and build the biological capacities for resilience.

Resilient people have what psychologists call "wobble," the ability to waver under the weight of life's suffering and trauma but not fall down.

Toxic stress, however, occurs when a child's stress response systems are activated in the absence of supportive, calming relationships, and stay activated for prolonged periods of time, when that's, "basically what life is usually like for a child. This is not the stress associated with a bad day. This is the stress associated with chronic activation of systems that disrupt brain circuits as they're developing, wears the body down."[97]

Resiliency

When we consider resiliency, we can refer to the myriads of research about the importance of resiliency factors in a growing child's life. One of the more humbling aspects of working in addiction treatment is to marvel at the resiliency and wobble of the clients who have survived tremendous trauma and deprivation, yet continue to return to treatment *one more time*, because they still have flickers of hope. This resiliency will be a vital resource in moving forward, and some residents will have it in greater amounts than others. Given our attachment focus in treatment, we will be building skills to assist residents to build in the relationships and support gained from others as part of their resiliency strategy.

I would encourage you to consider a small assessment such as the Responses to Stressful Experiences Scale (RSES), found in the APPENDIX) which is a 22-item scale emphasizing coping processes. It was developed by the NC-PTSD and was validated using active duty and reserve component military samples. It can provide a baseline for coping skills clients currently have gained and provide a roadmap for skills they could gain in the process of treatment.

3.2d Application example

Andre, a 34-year-old African American male, has recently been admitted to the treatment center directly after being arrested for public intoxication. He was already on probation, and the probation officer is hoping that treatment will help Andre change course in his life. This is the third treatment episode for Andre who is skeptical about treatment since he always drinks again when he completes his treatment and re-enters the community. However, his mother has convinced him to try one more time, so he has agreed to admission.

Andre presents as calm with a defensive posture. He is observational, quick-witted, and deflects attempts to learn more about his internal experiences and feelings. As part of his initial assessment his counselor, Brenda, will administer the ACEs study, and after he has completed it, will discuss his ACEs score and what it may mean to his ongoing struggle with sobriety.

"Andre, thanks for filling this out. It looks like you got a 5 on the study."

"It's what anyone who grew up in my neighborhood would put. I'm nothing special."

"Actually, I would say that given your number, you must have some serious survival skills to be sitting here, mostly intact!" Brenda gently smiles. She continues. "So, you say here that you were hit as a kid. Who hit you?"

"My Dad used to beat our ass when he got drunk. Only when he went to the bar, not when he drank at home. So, it could have been worse."

"And how often was that?"

"I don't know, never thought about it. Maybe once a week?"

"Did he hit your mom when he was hitting you?'

"Yeah, he was wild then. She would try to stand in front of my brother and me, and he'd hit her or push her away."

"That sounds pretty terrifying," Brenda offers, *"How old were you?"'*

"I hit him back when I was 13 and it stopped. So, it could have been worse."

"That's the second time you've said that, Andre. I take it you saw worse?"

"Yeah, I saw worse. At least my mom was home, and my Nana could watch us when Mom worked. We always had food on the table. Why are we talking about this, anyway? What does this have to do with my drinking?"

"That's a good question. This is the third time you've tried treatment, and it's important to me that we figure out the puzzle pieces we need to create a plan for you that will actually work this time. So, we're going to be giving you assessments like this, occasionally, trying to make sense out of what has happened in your life that has created strengths you can use and areas where you might need more tools or more support."

"So learning about my crappy childhood will help you figure out what's wrong with me?"

"I think of it more like looking at your history and figuring out your strengths and vulnerabilities. Honestly, I think your childhood and relationship history may have created some walls between you and other people; I can feel them when I am with you. That makes being part of your life kind of hard for people who care about you. Knowing more about your history also might help understand why AA hasn't worked for you. I'm hoping that over time you'll learn to think of people as part of your solution instead of surviving in spite of us – does that make sense?"

"I do alright by myself."

"Well, sort of. You're back in treatment again, so something isn't working. Research shows that people who can form stable relationships with other people, even two or three, seem to stay sober longer. I know you have your mom, so maybe you can figure out how to let at least two

more into your life at some point which will help you keep your sobriety this time. That's our theory.

    "They didn't talk about this stuff in treatment before."

"I know, but we have a different focus. I encourage you to try and keep an open mind. You might learn something," Brenda says with another smile.

"In fact, I am going to ask you to watch a YouTube video that I think will help you see where we're coming from, "Everything You Think You Know About Addiction is Wrong," by Johann Hari. While you're watching it, I want you to jot down some thoughts, and we'll talk about it when I see you for our next individual session in a couple of days. Thanks for being so open with me, Andre."

Chapter Four

4.1 Emotional Regulation

It is a helpful idea to introduce ways to address the hyperarousal and hypo arousal of the limbic system early in the process. Using tools for emotional regulation and distress tolerance is NOT the same as ignoring addiction or the depression. But we start where the client is ready – and the first source of pain is the entry point.

We can ask, *"Are you open to talking about other ways to manage your pain?"*

We can offer the resident options so that if, or when, they decide that substance use is not in their best interest, they have other ways to manage the pain that life brings and, maybe, different ways to form relationships.

We're talking about management, not elimination, of pain. If the suggestions don't work, we'll think of others.

Top-Down Processing

Traditional talk-based psychotherapy, and most cognitively oriented trauma-focused therapies, are viewed as taking a top-down approach to treatment. Most often this involves efforts to resolve trauma symptoms by working with the dorsolateral prefrontal cortex, the area of the brain most responsible for logic and reason.

Top-down processing presumes that something like a boss-employee relationship exists between the prefrontal cortex and the limbic system: namely, the thinking centers of the brain can activate cognitive controls adjusting the feeling centers of the brain.

Following this logic, enhanced cognitive regulation would enable a person to alter the relevance of current environmental "stimuli", things like:

- perceived and actual threats,
- trauma triggers and reminders,
- conflict, and
- stressors.

Over time, this would reshape a person's physiological and emotional responses to these experiences in the present.

Limitations of Top-Down Processing

Experimental research has demonstrated, however, that the brain's ability to regulate arousal through cognition becomes compromised, and can even be deactivated, by acute stress.

Otherwise, helpful cognitive capacities like perspective taking, reason, problem-solving and decision-making, and the capacity for impulse control routinely falter in the face of trauma. When the body's physiological alarm system is activated, the areas of the brain responsible for these higher order executive functions go dark.

When this occurs, our distinctively human cognitive controls stop working and cannot be recruited to shut down our more primitive "fight or flight" response or the many associated sensorimotor survival-driven action patterns that we have learned during past experiences of danger.

These survival-driven patterns get reactivated in the face of perceived threat, even when the current trigger is hardly life threatening and ultimately a false alarm, which is frustrating.

Co-Regulation

If you reflect back on our polyvagal discussion, remember that when first sensing danger, our autonomic nervous system looks for connection in order to find safety and regulation. This is impacted by our choices available to us in our response, and the context we find ourselves in. When we perceive unstable context, few choices and lack of connection a sense of unease develops, and our autonomic nervous system prepares for protection. We have a biological need for connection and a wired-in survival response. When they can both be engaged, we refer to this Co-regulation.

In relationships with another, for example. In a counseling session, the cues sent from one system to another can either co-regulate and invite new possibilities or increase reactivity and reinforce habitual survival patterns. We can utilize the counseling relationship as one of the key bridges to healing early attachment disruption patterns.

When we are co-regulated in our relationships, our ventral vagus nervous system is activated, and we are:

- Safe in our body
- Able to self-regulate
- Able to connect to self, others, the world
- Acknowledging our distress
- Exploring options
- Able to collaborate
- Reaching out for/offer support
- Resourceful

Healing the Body from the Bottom-Up

Other, more somatically driven and body-based interventions adopt what has been characterized as a bottom-up approach to trauma therapy. These interventions endeavor to undo trauma's imprint on the body by directly accessing the limbic system, the feeling center of the brain, and by directly targeting sensory receptors located throughout the body.

Bottom-up treatment interventions are believed by a growing number of complex trauma practitioners to regulate and adjust the visceral responses associated with complex trauma. This happens by resetting trauma-related emotional and sensory states stored within the limbic system and peripheral nervous system.

To activate this bottom-up process, the following activities could be used:

- exercise,
- rhythmic movement,
- deep, relaxed (diaphragmatic) breathing, and
- synchrony between breathing and heart rate

Proponents of traditional cognitive processing based treatment models insist that interventions that engage the body but do not explore traumatic memories directly cannot resolve symptoms of posttraumatic stress.

Compelling findings from well-designed studies of bottom-up interventions -- including trauma-sensitive yoga and clinical neurofeedback

-- for adults with long histories of limited response to traditional trauma therapies suggest otherwise.

Through the Side Door

Some visionary thinkers in the traumatic stress field, foremost among them Bessel van der Kolk, M.D., believe contemporary mind-body interventions engineer change by forging communication and restoring balance between the rational and emotional brain systems through a third pathway: the medial prefrontal cortex. This is what Dr. Joseph Spinazzola refers to as *the brain's secret side door.*

Neuroscience research findings based on advanced technology such as functional magnetic resonance imaging (fMRI) suggest that the limbic system can be consciously accessed through interoceptive awareness, a person's awareness and perception of the internal experience. It allows humans to integrate body sensations, thoughts and feelings.

In addition to mind-body approaches, participation in expressive arts-based interventions such as theater, storytelling and the visual arts, also seem to reach the medial prefrontal cortex through their drawing upon powerful cultural healing rituals and symbolism deeply rooted in the human experience which resonates with the human mind and spirit in a way transcending or at least circumventing the limits of logical thinking.

4.2 Emotional Regulation Strategies

We have a handful of senses built into our human experience that provide us with information about our environment. A common aspect of each of our senses is that they are occurring right now; they are part of our direct experience, not an abstract concept directed to the past or future. Thus, they have the power, when we are aware of them, to redirect our attention to our direct experience when we become preoccupied or agitated by thoughts. And they are always available to us.

If we want greater physical and emotional well-being and increase our emotional resilience, we can use sounds, feelings, sights, tastes, and smells to balance and heal ourselves.

CREATING THE SENSORY TOOL BOX

Sound

Clients can choose sounds from simple hometics sound machines to scrolling through YouTube to download MP3. They can go to a local music store that allows people to sample CDs through headphones before purchase. Encourage clients to take notes as they become aware of sounds they find comforting and make them available to use regularly. You could also consider integrating binaural sounds, such as Sooth the Nervouse System - Heal Your Vagus Nerve, Nerve Healing Binaural Beats - Nerve Regeneration.

Sights

Clients can spend time visiting art museums, viewing nature sights online, visit natural environments, looking through art books, architecture, and Mandala websites. Clients can visit paint stores and pick up paint swatches to learn more about color and their response to color. Clients can be encouraged to create collages using a variety of magazine images.

Smell

Clients can visit the scented oil displays at Whole Foods or other natural shops to experiment with smells and incense. They can spend time remembering favorite smells from childhood and pay attention to smells as they walk around in the world. Do they smell wood burning, freshly mowed grass, coconut oil from suntan lotion? Include these fragrances in their daily life routine in the form of candles, soaps, and oils.

Taste

Clients can experiment with new vegetables and fruits. Experiment with food prep using some of the food choices provided in this handout. Visit food stores to smell and taste various spices. Clients can experiment with various herbal teas and non-caffeinated beverages and create blended smoothies incorporating new tastes.

Touch

Encourage clients to experiment with various lotions, bath soaps and cremes they find comforting - more or less oily, soapy not soapy, etc.

Consider heated pads and blankets made of the fabrics discovered in the exercise below. Perhaps they can use exercises for physical pressure and movement. They may want to invest in a weighted blanket.

A TOUCH EXERCISE

Gather an assortment of fabrics and textures, examples would be fun fur, wool, silk, velour, tinsel, scrunched brown paper, bath scrunches, the list goes on. Search around your house and see what you can find lying around. Sit and hold your hand with your forearm facing upwards. Apply a firm amount of pressure and draw the fabric from the elbow to the wrist. Ask yourself if you like the texture. If you do, would they like more or less pressure? This is a simple case or trial and error, some people like scratchy textures whereas others love velour and like to start with very firm strokes and end lighter. Also try this on the cheeks, torso, back and legs. Once you have found the right texture and level of pressure, start using these fabrics to relax when stressed.

SAMPLE SENSORY TOOL BOX

I will share with you my toolbox as a sample. When I feel my adrenal system rising and notice that my shoulders are tensing, my chest feels hot, and I experience a slight tremor. Sometimes I find myself short of breath due to shallow breathing. I draw from the following sensory kit to help kick up my parasympathetic system and calm down

- I have a hometics sound machine, so I can turn on the ocean sounds
- Take off my shoes, and lay down on the squishy couch in my office
- I have a beaded tapestry on my wall of a cat watching koi fish, so I look at the wall hanging
- I light my favorite have a lilac and sandlewood candle
- I have a tied felt blanket my goddaughter made me I use if I am chilly or I can put my cat on my chest to feel the fur and feel the weight on my chest
- I close my eyes and listen to my breathing, and I can feel my system calming down.
- When I am ready to continue my day, I can make a cup of chamomile tea

Depending on the situation, I do not always need to use every single tool in my toolbox. But I have all the ingredients available if I need them.

Mindfulness to Repair the Brain

Brain scans of individuals who faced childhood adversity often show a loss of interconnectivity in areas that are critical to creating loving relationships, activating a sense of calm in the face of stress, and downshifting the inflammatory response. When these connections are underdeveloped, we have little awareness of our own feelings and lack of consciousness about the effects of our behavior on others. We cannot see how our defensive patterns of interacting are hurting those we care for; and we can't see how they are hurting us. We lack insight into how we can improve our relationships.

Mindfulness meditation helps us change our brain – and to bring the brain back online and reset out inflammation response.

Research shows that even though mindfulness practitioners still pump out inflammatory hormones such as cortisol when stressed, their cortisol levels go down more quickly once the stressor has passed. Faster cortisol recovery means you can rebound more quickly from stressful situations. It means that you reduce the time that your body and mind are bathed in inflammatory chemicals. This leads to less physical and neural inflammation and less physical disease, anxiety, and depression.

Sample Psychoeducation Training

Mindfulness Practice to Inhabit Your Body

When your mind has wandered in the midst of an activity or when lying in bed, use your senses to bring your awareness back into the here and now. More specifically, ask yourself, "What are five things that I hear, what are five things that I see, and what are five things that I feel?"

As an example, here is mindfulness a practice when taking a walk:

*"First, what are five things that you can **hear**? When you are walking, you almost always hear your feet clicking on the pavement, the sound of traffic, and birds singing. One thing you can always hear is your breath!"*

*"Second, what are five things you can **feel** on your body? The phone*

in your hand, the breeze on your cheeks, your feet in your shoes, and always, again, your breath going in and out."

*"Third, what five things can you **see**? Sometimes you can make it 'what five things can I see that are yellow,' maybe 'five types of leaf shapes,' 'five different flowers', 'how many colors blue or gray in the sky?' And if it's really cold, there it is again, your breath!*

What you may find is that when you are walking, you are paying no attention to your surroundings. Meanwhile, your head is spinning with worry and anxiety. Take a deep breath, listen, look and feel. Sometimes your mind wanders, but when it does, bring it back to what is happening right now, right here. It can be very helpful in reducing worry and to be more mindful in anything you do.

Chapter Five

5.1 Neurology Psychoeducation

It is normalizing for clients to have a glimpse into how their brain works as it is the primary organ that has been affected by their addiction and trauma! The goal of providing psychoeducation in these areas is to move the discussion of addiction from a stigmatizing character issue to a chronic medical condition. It also helps make the medication compliance argument to the client more relevant because co-occurring disorder is so prevalent in the trauma-affected population.

5.2 Stages of Change

Before leaving Phase One, it will be important to review the Stages of Change with the resident to assist them to determine their current stage of change. Keep in mind that the stage of change will fluctuate based on emotional regulation challenges. You will be having them complete the Readiness Ruler at the end of this phase and throughout the treatment episode in preparation for transition in the final phase of treatment.

The Transtheoretical Model (also called the Stages of Change Model), was developed by Prochaska and DiClemente in the late 1970s. The Transtheoretical Model (TTM) focuses on the decision-making of the individual and is a model of intentional change and operates on the assumption that people do not change behaviors quickly and decisively. Rather, change in behavior, especially habitual behavior, occurs continuously through a cyclical process. For each stage of change, different intervention strategies are most effective at moving the person to the next stage of change and subsequently through the model to maintenance, the ideal stage of behavior.

Stage I – Precontemplation:

- Unaware of the problem or greatly underestimates it
- Not thinking about changing.
- Actively resistant to the idea of change.
- No intention of changing within the next 6 months.
- Seeks help under pressure from others.

Stage II - Contemplation:

- Aware a problem exists.
- Thinking of changing, but ambivalent.
- Wants to change in the next six months but has no specific plan.
- Not yet made a commitment to action.
- Despite good intentions, may languish at this stage for a long time.

Stage III – Preparation:

- Has already made some unsuccessful change attempts.
- Thinking about change, intends to take action in the next month.
- Determines best method(s) for decisive action.
- Plans to change.

Stage IV – Action:

- Major behavioral change occurs now.
- Change is activated (for less than 6 months).
- The biggest risk is relapse.
- This stage requires considerable time and energy.

Stage V – Maintenance:

- Has been regularly practicing the change for 6 months or more.
- Continues to incorporate change into current lifestyle.
- Works to consolidate gains and prevent relapse.
- Remains free of problem behavior, with effective substitutes.

Stage VI – Termination:

- The change has been stable for at least one year.
- New self-image – new behavior and view of self are consistent. (Non-smoker)
- Lack of temptation – in any situation (no longer desire(s) to smoke, gamble, abuse food, alcohol, drugs, sex or any other target problem behavior).
- Solid self-efficacy – possesses a new genuine sense of self-confidence that they can function well without engaging in the former problem behavior.

- A healthier lifestyle – a way of living in which the old behavior plays no part in one's life.

- Staying in top psychological and spiritual shape – spends time and energy doing things that enhance self-growth, pursuing dreams, hanging out with healthier functioning people.

Ancillary Stage VII – Relapse/Recycling:

- A common occurrence which should be anticipated and resolved.

- Most relapsers do not give up.

- Research indicates only about 20% of the population make permanent changes on the first try.

- The majority of people fall back to the contemplation or preparation (not precontemplation) stage.

I have included a sample of the States of Change Readiness Ruler as a tool that can be used for a VARIETY of issues throughout the course of treatment. How ready are they to shift their attachment style? How ready are they to change their physical health? How ready are they to use the emotional regulation strategies we are recommending?

I would also recommend a Decision Balance sheet to provide a framework for residents to use as they learn to examine their own thinking.

The AIAT® model has a strong focus on assisting resident's tolerance for internal reflection, and using the emotional regulation skills we are offering to better maintain effective connections with others.

5.3 Readiness Ruler

Table 1:

0	1	2	3	4	5	6	7	8	9	10

Not ready for change   Ready for change

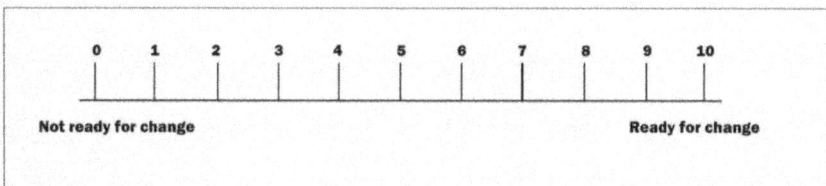

On a scale of 1 to 10, how important is it to you to make a change in...?
Example, If you are a 5, why are you a 5 and not a 3?
Or if you are a 5, what need to happen for you to go to a 7?
How could I assist you in getting to a 7?

Section Three:
Attachment Assessment and Skill Building: Phase Two

Chapter One

At this point in time, hopefully the resident has stabilized his/her withdrawal symptoms and is addressing any immune system damage, treatment interrupting psychiatric symptoms, and other physical consequences of ongoing substance abuse and nutritional neglect. There have also been two weeks of beginning attachment formation with the counseling staff and treatment program to allow the key shift from attachment to their drug of choice. They have had a chance to review the symptoms of addiction, their stage of change, considered the immune system impact of early childhood adversity and attachment interruption. At the end of this section, they will have completed their attachment style inventory and the Reflected Self-Functioning Questionnaire.

1.1 Attachment Style Assessment

It will be helpful to ask the Phase Two residents to complete an Attachment Style Questionnaire, and I would recommend This questionnaire is based on the Experience in Close Relationship (ECR) questionnaire.[101] The ECR was first published in 1998 by Kelly Brennan, Catherine Clark, and Phillip Shaver, the same Shaver who published the original "love quiz" with Cindy Hazan. Residents' will make a series of attachment-based questions, such as, "I find it easy to be affectionate with my partner," or " I find it difficult to depend on my partner." The more statements that you check in a category, the more you will display characteristics of the corresponding attachment style. Category A represents the *anxious* attachment style, Category B represents the *secure* attachment style, and Category C represents the *avoidant* attachment style.

1.2 Attachment Styles Strategies

Now that the residents have become familiar with the connection between attachment and addiction, it is an opportunity to deepen their opportunity to personalize the attachment theory and discover their attachment style. Using an Attachment Assessment, counselors can set aside time to sit with the resident as they complete the ECR assessment, and then discuss the attachment style that is revealed.

It is an opportunity to introduce the Attachment styles in more detail using the **Adult Attachment Styles** and then open a discussion about their personal attachment style and the styles they recognize in others close to them. If the resident is open to exploration, it would be helpful to make connections between their personal attachment style and the style of their early caregivers. Ideally, they can begin to see the multi-generational patterns that have contributed to their vulnerability to substance abuse disorder. The goal of pattern recognition is to reduce their internalized stigma, the cultural stigma toward addicts and alcoholics carried by addicts themselves.

Adult Attachment Style Strategies

Low Anxiety

Secure	Anxious
Want contact, but do not feel they need constant access Comfortable with more contact when needed and less contact when needed. Initiate contact when they feel it is necessary or if they feel like it. Always respond in a timely manner we possible Will communicate if they cannot.	**Want and need contact to feel loved and wanted.** Worry and feel anxious when there is less contact. Initiate contact because they are afraid the other person will not initiate ever again. Always respond when it is not needed or wanted. Respond to no contact with anxious behaviors including tantrums, stalking, lying, drive-bys, etc.
Avoidant	**Disorganized**
Do not need contact and resent anyone who expect it. Comfortable with less or no contact and can be slow to respond. Only respond when THEY feel it is necessary.	**Confused and anxious with requests for contact.** May want contact, but confused about how to achieve this. Confused when others initiate contact, unclear about the safety of responding, Response may not match the Initiation by the other.

High Avoidance

Counseling is the interplay between a resident's attachment style and the clinician's attachment style which creates a meaningful "learning lab." In this interchange residents can relive and modify historically meaningful patterns through the emotional relationship counseling offers as their attachment defenses and strategies surface. With the containment that empathy provides, the residents can develop a sense of mastery over previously frightening or forbidden feelings, leading to a greater capacity for self-soothing and awareness of more effective relational strategies.

Knowing the attachment styles and identifying their personal defensive strategies will be more effective with a shared attachment "language" or shorthand both in individual and group counseling. This requires the clinician to be aware of and be capable of managing their personal attachment style, being aware that their attachment defenses and strategies will also be at play. Counter-transference risks in the Attachment Infused Addiction Treatment® model are more readily identified, and the counseling staff will need to provide support and act as emotional regulation attachment figures in their working relationship with each other!

Rudi Dallos and Arlene Vetere have developed a systemic approach to addressing attachment and addiction.[102]

APPLICATION EXAMPLE

Brenda is meeting with Andre after he has had a chance to get involved in groups and see the YouTube video she recommended.

"So, Andre, when you first came in, we looked at your ACEs score, which was a 5, and we went through our ASAM assessment to look specifically at your drug and alcohol use. Do you remember that I said that I would be checking in with more assessments to keep creating a picture of your relationship strategies, and where you have strengths and where you need more tools?"

"Yes, I remember. I still don't see why stuff that happened so long ago matters now."

"Well, one of the things that can happen when you have a score like a 5, is that you may not have been able to feel secure with your parents – like they couldn't be a safety net for whatever reason. When we don't feel fully secure, we develop relationship strategies to stay safe, like either to avoid connecting or relying on people, or, if we do care about them, constantly trying to keep them from leaving. In both cases, we never really trust people will stay with us. Sometimes we were so afraid of caregivers that other people just don't feel safe to us. Can you picture this?"

"I think so. I know I feel better taking care of myself. I know my mom is always there, but I get smothered by her sometimes. She wants me to take care of her when she's sad, and I just can't take it."

"So, when you say 'better', do you mean less anxious?"

"What does anxious feel like? You guys use that term a lot."

"It means that sometimes when you start to feel worried or start scanning the room, might feel a little warm, your heart might speed us, your thoughts might start to race and you can't think, you –"

"Stop!" Andre, laughs, "I didn't know that's what it was called! I used to feel that way every time my girl would call. She'd call and call. I just couldn't answer the phone."

"Have you felt that way since you have been here?"

"Dude, I feel that way every time we have to check in for group. I hate that shit! It's none of anyone's business how I'm feeling."

Brenda laughs. "I'm going to ask you to take an attachment assessment to see if we can find out how close you let people get to you. Then we'll go over your score, ok?"

Chapter Two

2.1 Shifting the Focus to Current Attachment Opportunities

Beyond establishing the counseling relationship as a secure base, Dallos and Vetere[103] suggest a focus on exploring – identifying attachment dilemmas and ambivalence in their current relationships such as *attachment threats, attachment fears, attachment injuries, attachment longings, and divided loyalties.* These are all key triggers to a return to substance use. Empathic failures, inevitable in the treatment context, provide the opportunity to be worked through and repaired.

The greater the frequency that ruptured bonds with the counseling staff and therapeutic group can be repaired, the stronger the ability of the resident to trust the attachment will be. This will require clinicians to respond non-defensively even in the face of narcissistic injuries created by the dismissive and rejecting responses of an avoidant or anxious, or disorganized recovering addict. Ideally, our residents will be internalizing the emotional regulation skills we demonstrate as we offer the tolerance of conflict their early attachment did not offer.

It will be important to assist the clients to retrieve memories and feelings that have been defensively excluded and reframing these experiences as adaptive responses to a signal of danger, separation, threat of separation, or unreliability in attachment relationships. Much like substance abuse counseling, we need to separate behavior from character. We can draw upon Allen Shores' work on affect regulation which states that **"the goal of attachment-focused treatment is to restructure strategies of affect regulation."**[104] We can then assist residents to think about what attachment strategies he is presently using in the interactions with his current important attachment figures. Patricia Crittenden, the Dynamic Maturational Model, suggests that we need to enable the resident to apply the right self-protective strategies at the right time in the right context. Rather than eliminate secure, anxious or avoidant strategies, we learn to apply them in the right relational situation.

Effective treatment is based on the implied notion that the essence of being human is social, not individual. The long-term goal of treatment is helping the substance abuser develop the capacity for mutuality and attachment, which helps break the substance abuser's cycle of alienation and isolation. *"Careful consideration needs to be given to providing enough emotional gratification to keep alcoholics and addicts in treatment while helping them accept their diagnosis and "acculturating them into the culture of recovery."*[105]

Group counseling, as the primary counseling intervention, offers an opportunity to increase attachment recognition and attachment-interfering behaviors in a safe container. In fact, individual therapy can seem too intense due to the heightened visibility and risk of dependency feelings in an intimate setting. The intensity is reduced and spread out in group therapy. The group provides a holding environment, allowing the recovering addict to achieve an emotionally mutual dependent relationship with other group members without being hijacked by therapy interfering attachment strategies. Flores[106] points out that group cohesion is to group therapy what the therapeutic alliance is to individual therapy.

In reference to the Twelve Step groups specifically, Lewis and his colleagues,[107] note that the limbic regulation in a group can restore balance to its members, allowing them to feel centered and whole. The shared narratives between fellow addicts serve to firm up the attachment bond.

APPLICATION EXAMPLE

Brenda is meeting with Andre after his Attachment Style Assessment.

"OK, Andre, I think neither one of us is surprised when I say you scored as more avoidant in your relationship style," Brenda says with a smile.

"That means I don't let people get too close to me, right?"

"Right, in fact when they try it might make you anxious or uncomfortable."

"Got that right! So what? What does that have to do with drinking?"

"I wonder if you ever noticed if your drinking goes up or down when you're with people."

"It always goes up; it loosens me up. But that's true of a lot of people."

"It is. But most people can stop after one or two drinks; they don't want to get too loose. You don't drink like that, I would guess."

"No, I guess I don't."

"One of the reasons we try to figure out what kind of attachment style you have is that helps us figure out the kinds of relationship situations that might threaten you, trigger your anxiety, or even hurt your feelings. It matters because a lot of people, including you I suspect, drink or use more when they feel uncomfortable or anxious with other people."

"I'm okay with people as long as they stay out of my business."

"What if your business is trying to stay sober? That would mean you wouldn't be willing to talk to a sponsor in A.A., or trust me, your counselor, while you're here. So, when you leave here you won't have any new skills to make healthy relationships out there – see what I mean?"

"Why do I have to have other people? Why can't I just stay sober by myself?"

"Well, you tried that several times. But like most avoidant people, sooner or later you get lonely and then someone gets over your wall. When they do, you get really anxious, right?"

"You might be right. I never thought about it that way."

"If the theory holds, it means that sooner or later your anxiety will make you push her away which will hurt, and you might drink more. Right?"

"Yeah, I can see it."

"So, our goal is to help you manage your discomfort as you begin to let people in so that you can begin to experience people as helpful and not hurtful. You can create a small support system- not 500 Facebook friends – just 3 people you feel safely connected to so you can break this pattern.

"They will keep me from drinking?"

"Well, it also takes using the skills to manage your emotions, challenging your thinking when it gets a little paranoid, and making good decisions that treat you like you matter."

"So, how am I supposed to do that?"

"You're going to have to learn how to listen to yourself and the clues your body, thoughts, and emotions give you about what you need and how to take care of yourself."

2.2 Addressing Meaning and Alienation

The attraction of using a substance is that you know what you are going to feel and when you are going to feel it. It offers the possibility of control and the capacity for denial and avoidance that no human relationship can but exacerbates the sense of emptiness and internal void.

As Edward Khantzian said in his Foreword to Philip Flores seminal work, *Addiction As A Attachment Disorder*, *"The worst fate, however is not the suffering; [of the addict} The worst fate is suffering alone."* What if the real task of therapy is as Eric Fromm suggested, *"essentially an attempt to help the patient gain or regain his capacity for love."*[108]

Jason Wright emphasizes the importance of "differentiation between human suffering at the root of using and the struggles with the substance." This does not diminish the importance of the disease of addiction and its accompanying neurological changes. It suggests that we need to address the disease in two layers simultaneously, both of which require the forming of an effective attachment relationship.

Research indicates that the deprivation of developmental needs can result in vulnerabilities that in turn lead to misguided attempts at self-repair, leaving the individual "constantly searching for something 'out there' that can be substituted for what is missing 'in there'."[109] The activating and stimulating action of drugs such as cocaine help such individuals break through their impoverished or diminished sense of self to "connect" to others; otherwise they are unable to. However, stimulant users speak of the pseudo-intimacy the drug provides, referring to such interactions as "speed talk."

Working with addicts means that we will frequently witness the lack of self-care and self-abandonment that leads them into risky and dangerous situations. This can reflect an attitude that *"Since no one cares what happens to me or wants to protect me, (I) it doesn't matter."*

Chapter Three

3.1 Reflexive Self-Function

Integration involves reconsidering one's experience, both past and present, from multiple perspectives to gain an understanding of what one has experienced, how one has used that experience to develop self-protective strategies, the influence of change in oneself and one's context, and finally one's emerging ability to regulate the process of development in the future through increased self-reflective capacities.

After identifying the attachment areas of concern, it's important to explore alternate perceptions and behaviors, promoting change, and supporting relational and emotional risk taking in real time. Acknowledging the risks of change and the threats to the perceptions of self and others loosens the attachment dilemmas. The goal is to develop the resilience to stay connected to others when there are ruptures and conflicts to maintain the long-term relations necessary for ongoing sobriety.

It's important to develop a resident's capacity for reflection to develop a more balanced, coherent narrative of self-and others in relational situations without getting lost in their own arousal system. As recovering addicts gradually recover their previously diminished cognitive functioning, alternate treatment strategies can be implemented once their capacity for new learning, consolidation of information, abstract thought, creative thinking, and motivation have all returned to their premorbid level. *At that point addicts can utilize insight, self-understanding, and autonomous decision-making skills.*[110]

3.2 Reflexive Functioning Questionnaire (RFQ)

It is helpful to use Fonogy's Reflective Self-Functioning Questionnaire[111] to introduce this vital cognitive shift. To review, Fonogy and colleagues found a strong relationship between attachment styles and a person's capacity to think about oneself in relation to others. They called this ability the reflexive self-function (RSF) which reflects a person's capacity for inner speech and insight.

The RSF is imbedded in the Adult Attachment Inventory (AAI). The scales for the AAI were based on the maxims for discourse established by the philosopher Paul Grice.[112] Grice's maxims described appropriate discourse under the constraints of a social situation. These maxims addressed four dimensions of cooperation between speakers in a conversation. The first dimension is **Quantity**, providing sufficient information to answer the question asked. **Quality** refers to providing accurate information, supporting any assertions made, and an absence of conflicting data. **Relevance** refers to staying on topic. The final dimension, **Manner,** refers to the clarity and coherence of the explanations given.

Transcripts of insecurely attached individuals tend to demonstrate a loss of self-regulation that interferes with verbal expression.[113] Transcripts that are classified as 'anxious' exhibit violations of verbal exchanges in the form of passive language or angry language that reduces their overall scores for coherence. Similarly, transcripts that are classified as 'avoidant' exhibit violations of verbal exchanges due to inconsistencies or lack of support for their statements. Scores for scales measuring avoidant characteristics reflect the use of defensive strategies, such as inability to recall childhood, derogation of attachment figures, or idealization of parents. However, even transcripts judged to be secure are likely to demonstrate preoccupied or dismissing features at low levels.

It is hopeful to remember that in spite of the stability of attachment patterns, some adults appear to earn security in their adult relationships.[114] Although these adults may describe their childhood attachment experiences as negative, they are able to do so in the coherent, balanced, and implicitly forgiving manner that is consistent with those who are categorized as securely attached.[115] They also demonstrate capacities for clarity in placing their history in the past by self-monitoring their narrative. They do not become lost in the past or seem unaware of inconsistencies between the details (semantic memory) of the narrative and the account of the total event (episodic memory).

In an effort to establish the resident's current capacity for explicit reflexive self-reflection, it will be helpful early in Phase Two to begin to explore the resident's capacity for *Explicit Reflexive Functioning, which is a state in which individuals are able to explicitly think and speak about mental states.*[106]

Specifically, we will assess the level of genuine mentalizing ability, which is characterized by demonstrating a moderate certainty about the mental states of oneself and others, while at the same time grasping the fact that mental states are complex and sometimes partially inaccessible to us.[116]

Clinicians could choose to utilize the Reflexive Functioning Questionnaire (RFQ), though it was originally normed on severely attachment disrupted clients, such as Borderline Personality Disorder. The RFQ measures reflexive functioning tendencies measured in the RSFQ scale, such as **Hypomentalizing.** Psychic equivalence mode, also known as hypomentalizing, is a mental mode in which individuals equate their outer reality with their inner mental reality.[117] Because this is seldom the case, *individuals with this tendency are often intolerant of other alternative perspectives,* which in turn leads to an uncertain reflexive style characterized by individuals having concrete, rigid understandings of mental states. This uncertain style often causes these individuals to *refrain from attempting to mentalize.* Even though individuals possessing an uncertain reflexive style are sometimes aware of their limitations when it comes to understanding themselves and others, this is often not the case.[118]

On the other end of the Likert scale is the **Hypermentalizing** mode. The pretend mode, also known as hypermentalizing, is a mental mode characterized by certainty when it comes to reflexive functioning.[119] Ideas often form no relationship between outer and inner reality, so that *an individual's mental representations are missing a link to the external reality.* The certain reflexive style includes the creation of mental representations of actions, while lacking satisfactory evidence to support the representations. The development of inaccurate models of the reflexive functioning of others and oneself can often be recognized by others as *long-winded and overly detailed statements that have little or no apparent relationship to outer, testable reality*. Based on the vast amount of reflexive output, the certain style often makes these individuals believe they are "good mentalizers". This often results in biased responses on self-report assessment tools assessing reflexive functioning.[120] *This mode is often characterized by meaninglessness, emptiness and dissociation* as a consequence of trauma, and can often be perceived as protracted talk about feelings and thoughts. These conversations are often *lacking an emotional component*.[113]

The goal of taking the RFQ is to identify evidence of resident hypomentalizing (intolerance of other's perspectives and avoiding other's perspectives) to hypermentalizing, which is evidenced by hyper-attention to their own internal reality, without strong connection to external reality. Both ends of the continuum interrupt a resident's capacity for perspective taking, empathy, identification with fictitious characters, and awareness of their own personal distress. These qualities are essential for strong attachment formation, and means we can foster the development of those specific abilities while simultaneously supporting the development of general reflective capacities.

APPLICATION EXAMPLE

Brenda is now meeting with Andre after he has completed the AIAT® Reflexive Functioning Questionnaire.

SCORING THE AIAT® ADAPTED RFQ

The Adapted RFQ, used in the AIAT® model, is to used for **general understanding** to gather a sense of a high or low ability to see the perspective and emotional state of others vs themselves. I have included the review of the RFQ tendencies for counselor scoring to draw a conclusion about the resident's ability to accurately understand themselves and others.

Rate 1 to 7

1. __ People's thoughts are a mystery to me. (High number = Hypermentalizing)

2. __ I don't always know why I do what I do. (High number = Hypomentalizing)

3. __ When I get angry, I say things without really knowing why I am saying them. (High number = Hypomentalizing)

4. __ When I get angry, I say things that I later regret. (High number = Hypermentalizing)

5. __ If I feel insecure, I can behave in ways that put others' backs up. (High number = Hypomentalizing)

6. __ Sometimes I do things without really knowing why. (High number = Hypomentalizing)

7. __ I always know what I feel. (High number = Hypermentalizing)

8. __ Strong feelings often cloud my thinking. (High number = Hypermentalizing)

Andre scored a 3 for Hypermentalizing, and 8 for Hypomentalizing. This means he tends to be inflexible in this thinking and has not been interested in his internal reality.

Brenda begins. *"Hey Andre, I wanted to look at your RFQ with you. You're an interesting dude. It looks like you haven't paid a lot of attention to what's going on inside of you, but you seem to get distressed or react when you get around other people's strong emotions. I wonder if this means it surprises you, and catches you off guard, when you lose it?"*

"What do you mean?"

"I wonder if the reason you avoid getting involved with others is because you get triggered when other people have strong feelings. Maybe it makes you so uncomfortable you want to bolt."

"Well, I told you about my Mom. She's too much, man."

"Do you ever feel that way here – maybe in groups?"

"Like when Maricela started to cry in group? Man, I thought you should have DONE something – you just let her cry. That's harsh."

"So, you assume that Maricela was as upset as YOU were feeling. What if she was feeling something different?"

"Like what? I mean, she was crying, so she was upset."

"Is it possible that when people cry they are not as upset as YOU would be if YOU were crying?"

"Really?"

"It might be interesting for you to ask her sometime. So, what did you do when I didn't "do something" and let her cry?"

"Honestly, I just checked out."

"What if I told you that I'm genuinely interested in feedback about how I'm doing? That I want you to say something if you get uncomfortable?"

"I'd say that I don't believe you."

"Andre, have you seen other people push back on me?"

"Yeah."

"And what happened?"

"Actually, you took it pretty well. You didn't agree, but you didn't lose your shit, either."

"That sounds about right. Why would I respond differently to you?"

"Hmm. I don't know."

"My challenge is for you to let me know when you're getting triggered. My goal is to help you figure out how to stay connected to me EVEN THOUGH I'm triggering you, and help you not have to check out. Do you remember the mindfulness skills we have been talking about? You know, when you get triggered to check out you can start naming the objects in the room in your head, or see how many smells you smell in the room, start listening for sounds in the room, feel the fabric of your jeans with your hands. . .

"Why do I need to learn about this?"

"Because if you can learn to stay present when you get uncomfortable, it helps you be able to think and make better choices for yourself in your relationship with other people. You get to respond instead of react."

"OK. We'll see."

"Also, I encourage you to be curious about what other people might be REALLY thinking and feeling rather than assume they feel and think like you do. You might find it interesting."

"How would I do that?"

"You could try asking them what they are feeling," Brenda says with a smile.

3.3 Metacognitive Skill Development

There are basic metacognitive skills that our residents can develop to strengthen their capacity to participate in secure attachment relationships and maintain them in their recovery. We'll return to authors Daniel P. Brown and David S. Elliott in *Attachment Disturbances in Adults,* [121] for **guidelines for reflective metacognitive skill development**.

1. Basic MetAwareness of the state of mind of self and others.

2. Monitoring the accuracy of state of mind.

3. Awareness of one's own influence on the other's state or behavior, and vice versa.

4. Becoming aware of one's state of mind in such a way that it has a regulatory effect on them.

5. Awareness of one's own or another's action plans and goal directedness.

6. Meaning-making.

Higher metacognitive skills

1. Recognition of how the past shapes one's experiences.

2. Appreciating the relativity of states of mind.

3. Seeing beyond information given, more deeply into underlying assumption and expectancies related to the information.

4. Optimizing action plans in the face of accurate awareness of limitations.

5. Fostering sensitivity to contextual effect on behaviors.

6. Perspective-taking, or the ability to consider something from another's point of view.

3.4 Attachment Based Addiction Treatment Model Metacognitive Treatment Planning Goals:

When we review the range of metacognitive skills, we can see clear treatment planning goals for the Attachment Infused Addiction Treatment® model:

1. Accurate recognition of their emotions

2. Accurate recognition of the emotions in others.

3. Being able to accurately feel what it would be like to be in that person's position.

4. Based on the above, being able to adjust their own behavior accordingly to achieve strengthened attachments with members of their support system.

Number four, ability to adjust their own behavior accordingly to achieve strengthened attachments with members of their support system, opens the door to expressing greater emotional intelligence, or EQ, skills.

3.5 Emotional Quotient (EQ) Skills

Emotional intelligence (otherwise known as emotional quotient or EQ) is the ability to understand, use, and manage your own emotions in positive ways to relieve stress, communicate effectively, empathize with others, overcome challenges and defuse conflict. Emotional intelligence is commonly defined by four attributes:

Self-management – Ability to control impulsive feelings and behaviors, manage your emotions in healthy ways, take initiative, follow through on commitments, and adapt to changing circumstances.

Self-awareness – Recognize your own emotions and how they affect your thoughts and behavior. You know your strengths and weaknesses and have self-confidence.

Social awareness – Empathy. You can understand the emotions, needs, and concerns of other people, pick up on emotional cues, feel comfortable socially, and recognize the power dynamics in a group or organization.

Relationship management – Knowing how to develop and maintain good relationships, communicate clearly, inspire and influence others, work well in a team, and manage conflict.

Developing stronger Emotional Intelligence skills lends itself to a Psychoeducation group, with opportunities to practice these skills in the residential milieu. Simple skills could include,

1. Reflect on your own emotions

2. Ask others for perspective.

3. Be observant (of your own emotions).

4. Use "the pause" (e.g., taking a moment to think before speaking).

5. Explore the "why" (bridge the gap by taking someone else's perspective).

6. When criticized, don't take offense. Instead, ask, "What can I learn?"

As you work with the residents to determine their self-reflective strengths and difficulties, it is a good time to offer a variety to skill-building exercises to develop both emotional and cognitive recognition and a vocabulary to share their internal world.

Chapter Four

4.1 ASAM Dimension Treatment Planning for Attachment and Addiction

We have spent considerable time in assessment of addiction, medical condition, co-occurring symptoms, reflexive functioning, resiliency, ACE's, attachment styles, metacognitive skills, and Stage of Change. This can provide an overwhelming amount of data, and it is important to keep the information within the ASAM Dimensions outline to make sense to us and more importantly, the client.

Keeping in mind that the heart of the ASAM is individualized treatment planning, there are some re-occurring issues that might be helpful to keep in mind.

Dimension I: Acute Intoxication and/or Withdrawal Potential

Withdrawal symptoms will manifest based on whether the drugs themselves are stimulants or depressives. If the resident is addicted to opiates, (parasympathetic system) benzodiazepines, or alcohol, then his withdrawal will be sympathetic in nature, which means elevation of heart rate, sweating, goosebumps, nausea, etc. If in alcohol or benzodiazepine withdrawal, these sympathetic symptoms could elevate into stroke or seizure and require immediate intervention.

It is at this juncture that resident history will be vital, as there needs to be a decision to introduce medication management for stabilization and craving management if indicated. Depending on complicating mental health or other medical conditions, the withdrawal phase may extend for several weeks, so the goal is increased functioning over time to enable the resident to participate in treatment even if program structure needs to be modified to accommodate the resident's withdrawal and stabilization process. Even attending one group a day facilitated by the Peer counselor begins the process of relationship engagement with the other residents.

The Peer counselor assigned to the resident needs to enter the treatment episode from the beginning of the withdrawal process. It is helpful to pair the Peer relationship with increased physical wellness to enable attachment-disrupted clients to begin to experience another person with healing. The Peer will follow this client over the next year, so the earlier this pairing begins the better.

Dimension 2: Biomedical Conditions and Complications: Additional medical conditions potentially interfering in treatment participation.

Addiction is a biochemical, biological disorder, and addressing the physical impact of years of substance use, trauma, and chronic stress has left its trace at the cellular level. Apart from the immediate withdrawal symptoms, we will need to provide the opportunity to identify other physical issues which need attention.

Attachment-disrupted residents have a history of hyperfocusing on their physical symptoms if anxiously attached, or being disengaged or minimizing physical symptoms if avoidant or disorganized attached. Self-report of health condition status may not be reliable.

This indicates a need for a full physical examination with a full blood panel, as well as prioritizing currently known medical conditions that need to be stabilized or evaluated (diabetes, hypertension, bone density changes). It is not uncommon for prior physical therapy or medication regimens to have been abandoned or medical follow-ups forgotten. If residents are entering with current medication for medical conditions, it is important to have the dosages assessed and adjusted if they have been evaluated for mental or physical conditions while abusing substances.

The presence of ongoing chronic stress of the addiction lifestyle, as well as likely early trauma, suggests that we have additional blood work that checks the immune system, which ideally includes immunoglobulin levels in the blood, protein electrophoresis, T (thymus derived) lymphocyte count, white blood cell count, and (cortisol)adrenocorticotropic hormone (ACTH) to establish a medical baseline.

Given the likely ongoing adrenal stress and calcium leeching from drug metabolism, it might be helpful to consider nutrition planning and even supplements to help support the residents to heal and shore up their depleted systems.

Dimension 3: Emotional, Behavioral or Cognitive Conditions and Complications

The ASAM will ask about prior mental health treatment, history with violence and suicide attempts, psychiatric interventions, and current mental health symptoms. In fact, this would be a good time to consider the use of the short form of the mental status exam. However, some drugs can lead to prolonged or protracted withdrawal, lasting for months and sometimes up to a year. People who consume a large amount of an intoxicating substance for a long time are more likely to develop Post Acute Withdrawal symptoms which can last from six months to a year and can mimic long-standing mental health conditions. These symptoms can include sudden mood swings, cognitive distortions, insomnia, irritability and reactivity, poor concentration, and fatigue. Given the potential for confusion, and poor self-observation, it will be important to locate outside records of prior treatment and to ascertain whether mental health conditions were identified when the client was actively using substances. This can take time to sort out, which is one of the reasons for the extended stay in treatment recommendation in the Attachment Infused Addiction Treatment® model.

The focus of the Attachment Infused Addiction Treatment® will add the resident's attachment style strategies, metacognition skills, reflexive functioning skills, and emotional regulation skills. Because these are not traditionally included in substance use treatment plans, I have created some suggested treatment planning ideas.

Sample Attachment Style strategies to include in treatment planning:

Problem: Resident distances from recovery support when feeling vulnerable, which interferes with use of recovery support system.

Goal: Identify attachment strategies that create distance when beginning to feel close to someone and practice tolerating small amounts of closeness.

Action Plan: Resident will identify three individuals in treatment milieu with whom to practice emotional honesty, and practice use of developing attachment skills. Will report progress to primary counselor weekly.

Problem: Resident demonstrates disruptive emotional escalation behaviors to demand attention when perceiving others as emotionally unavailable, which alienates recovery support and leads to isolation.

Goal: Identify reactive attachment strategies used when you perceive the other person has become emotionally unavailable and decrease escalation behaviors.

Action: Resident will keep a daily log tracking feelings of anxiety and desire to escalate and identify perceived behaviors in others that are triggering. Resident will share log daily with their Peer Counselor.

Problem: When resident perceives emotional threat, they involuntarily dissociate and becomes unable to utilize recovery support or emotional regulation skills to remain available for sober relationships.

Goal: Identify dissociative attachment strategies employed when triggered or over-stimulated and utilize mindfulness strategies.

Action: Resident will utilize relaxation strategies three times a day to allow him/her to monitor rising internal distress and keep a daily journal of triggers as they are identified. Resident will share journal with primary counselor once a week.

Problem: Resident does not ask for help when needed in treatment milieu, which interferes in his/her ability to fully participate in treatment groups and disconnects them from recovery support.

Goal: Take opportunities to allow others to be of emotional or practical assistance by asking for help.

Action: Resident will take one opportunity a day to ask one other person in milieu for either emotional or practical assistance and keep a log in his journal to share with his primary counselor once a week.

Sample metacognitive skills I have mentioned include:

Problem: Resident lacks the emotional vocabulary to accurately identify their emotions as they arise and then effectively communicate them, which prevents effective use of recovery support.

Goal: Resident will increase emotional vocabulary and effectively communicate these emotions to others in the treatment milieu.

Action: Resident will review "feeling faces" sheet during daily check in with his/her Peer Counselor and accurately communicate feelings to them.

Problem: Resident unable to accurately identify emotions in others, which leads to inappropriate responses and disconnects them from recovery support.

Goal: Increase ability to accurately recognize emotions in others and reflect them more accurately and consistently to facilitate recovery support.

Action: Resident will identify two people in each process group each week to practice reflecting on the emotions they are hearing from the speaker and ask them if you are hearing them accurately.

Problem: Resident unable to accurately see situations from another person's perspective, which creates cognitive inflexibility and distances them from recovery support.

Goal: Increase ability to accurately feel and understand what it would be like to be in another person's position, increasing ability to form ongoing recovery support.

Action: Resident will select three people in the treatment milieu as "practice partners" and practice reflecting "So, from your perspective..." at least once a day for each. Resident will keep a log of these "practice sessions" and share with Peer counselor daily.

Problem: Resident is unable to adjust their behavior in social situations to accommodate the needs to others, which interrupts his/her ability to maintain recovery support.

Goal: Develop the ability to adjust their behavior when necessary to achieve strengthened attachments with members of their support system.

Action: Resident will choose three people in the treatment milieu to practice trusting to provide him/her accurate feedback about how the resident's behavior is affecting others and adjust the behavior accordingly. Resident will keep a log of this feedback and share with his/her primary counselor weekly.

Sample increased resiliency skills might include:

Problem: Resident quickly disengages from tasks when encountering roadblocks, which prevents him/her from completing important recovery tasks that will lead to ongoing sobriety.

Goal: Increase sense of self-efficacy when encountering difficulties.

Action: Resident will complete "Cognitive Distortion" worksheet, and practice challenge statements that allow them to continue towards problem solving.

Problem: Resident's cognitive rigidity when encountering problems interferes with their ability to engage in effective problem-solving strategies and disengages them from the treatment milieu.

Goal: Residents will increase ability to view problems from at least two other perspectives, which will allow them to more effectively match solutions to problem viewpoint.

Action: Resident will practice looking at a problem at least three different ways and identify solutions and consequences that would match the view of the problem. Resident will keep a log of the three different views and share with his/her Peer counselor weekly.

Sample Reflexive Functioning goal:

Problem: Resident is unable to verbalize or access thoughts and ideas without becoming overwhelmed by their arousal system and then shutting down ability to receive recovery support.

Goal: Increase capacity for reflection of accurate verbal expression without getting overwhelmed by personal arousal system.

Action: Resident will increase ability to monitor elevating arousal responses by utilizing the biofeedback training three times a week with Peer counselor.

Dimension 4: Readiness to Change

I have indicated the use of the Readiness Ruler, and I strongly encourage psychoeducation about the Stages of Change to encourage the residents to identify their stage of change as it shifts over time. If we remember that substances are a secure attachment source that has replaced unavailable caretakers, it makes sense that the stakes are even higher to the resident when they consider shifting this attachment. The strength of the addictive craving combined with the early use of substances for self-soothing would indicate that we will need to re-evaluate readiness to change as they begin to attempt to form trusted attachments with the Peer counselor, primary counselor, and other residents.

The key idea in this dimension is to match the intensity of the intervention with the resident's willingness to change and stage of change. It will be important to normalize their fear and resistance, and return to the question, "What did the substance DO for you? What purpose does it serve?" Remind them that, "*We're talking about management, not elimination, of pain. If the suggestions don't work, we'll think of others.*"

To assess for substance use readiness to change, you may want to add the Readiness to Change Questionnaire (Treatment Version) (RCQ-TV) (Revised) or the Stages of Change Readiness and Treatment Eagerness Scale (SOCRATES) found in the SAMHSA TIP 35 manual as a treatment plan item:

Explore readiness to change my substance use by completing the Readiness to Change Questionnaire and share the results with my counselor.

Cooccurring Disorders: It is highly probable that many of our clients will have either previously diagnosed mental health disorders or will be demonstrating evident symptoms of mental health disorders in addition to SUD.

Readiness to Change can be vastly different between willingness to address mental health versus substance use, and ASAM Dimension 4 may need to be revisited multiple times throughout the treatment episode to match treatment plan goals and actions plans with stage of change for each issue.

Readiness to Change may also vary between willingness to shift attachment style and addiction.

Dimension 5: Relapse, Continued Use, or Continued Problem Potential

Just as readiness to change varies between attachment strategies, substance use, and mental health disorders, so does relapse potential. The focus is on how mental health, substance craving, and attachment disruption will lead to relapse into substance use behavior. This dimension has a focus on the resident's ability to utilize previous relapse prevention strategies or may indicate they lack the relapse prevention skills required to function at a lower level of care.

The Attachment Infused Addiction Treatment® model folds in social skill development and social network mapping to develop a social support map for ongoing recovery. In this model, we will include the Social Network Mapping as a foundation for relapse prevention. It is a given that the residents attending this model may have been exposed to traditional relapse triggers and craving management psychoeducation in previous treatment episodes and may have been able to use those skills for short periods of time after leaving treatment. However, inability to incorporate support and develop mutual relationships leads to decreased ability to manage emotional reality and a return to substances for self-soothing.

Treatment planning will include items such as

- I will map my social network and share this map with my counselor.
- I will complete my Relapse Prevention plan to include new prevention strategies and share with my outside support group prior to transition from residential treatment.

Dimension 6: Recovery/Living Environment

We will need to examine the resident's living and social support options as they prepare to leave treatment. One of the possible assessment tools we use is the MIRC- Multidimensional Inventory of Recovery Capital Adapted for AIAT® Based on research tool designed by Bowen, E. Irish, A. Wilding, G., LaBarre, C., Cappozziello, Nochajski, T. ,Granfield, R. & Kaskutas, L. (2023) MIRC- Multidimensional Inventory of Recovery Capital. I have included this in the APPENDIX.

Our primary focus in this dimension is the Attachment Infused Addiction Treatment® model includes taking the Social Network map and developing a Recovery Village, which includes specific people who will play specific roles in their lives at the next level of treatment. The support people will be listed with contact phone numbers on one sheet for easy portability.

The resident will need to identify an ongoing structure for their time, and clearly identify opportunities to practice the metacognitive, reflexive, resilience, and emotional intelligence skills they have been practicing in the residential level of care. This includes time with the Peer counselor weekly, attendance at mutual support groups, and partial hospitalization or intensive outpatient levels of care.

Treatment planning will include:

- I will complete my Recovery Village and share with my outside support group prior to transition from residential care.
- I will create a weekly schedule will meetings, work, and other meetings clearly identified with relevant location and phone data.

Section Four:
Identifying Secure Attachment Options: Phase Three

Chapter One

The focus of the third phase is to solidify the belief that people can be part of their recovery solution. The path to future emotional regulation is in their secure and trusted attachments and not their drug of choice.

We have spent Phase One and Two exploring the impact of early attachment disruption on the resident's ability to develop the support necessary for long-term recovery. We have connected early attachment disruption to attachment to substances and the reality of addiction on their lives. They have become clear about the immune system and neurological impact of attachment damage on the hypo and hyperarousal systems. They have been practicing effective self-soothing skills when recognizing the fight, flight, or freeze responses to triggers. Residents have been practicing new metacognitive strategies for more effective communication and connections and have begun to establish the belief that trust MIGHT be possible going forward. **Hopefully, they have begun to demonstrate four markers of increased self-reflection skills:**

1. Accurate recognition of their emotions.

2. Accurate recognition of the emotions in others.

3. Being able to accurately feel what it would be like to be in another person's position.

4. Based on the above, be able to adjust their own behavior accordingly to achieve strengthened attachments with members of their recovery support system.

Our attention now turns to relapse prevention and discharge planning. In reality, we have had an eye on discharge planning from early ASAM assessment and have been addressing relapse prevention throughout the course of treatment as triggers to use are revealed. However, it is time to pull together formal relapse prevention planning from an attachment-based vantage point, identifying ongoing impediments to forming the vital support necessary for long-term recovery.

1.1 Conceptualizing social support and social integration

We need to identify the attachment and support options in their immediate world at varying levels of intimacy. We need to assist the client to create a tangible reminder of the supports available to them when they become triggered after they transition to the next level of care.

Although sometimes used interchangeably with terms such as *social integration, social networks,* or *social relationships,* a narrower definition of *social support* is also common. [122] In that narrower usage, *social support* refers to social interaction in which the actions of one party are intended to benefit another party. Thus, though social support may be seen as one aspect of other, broader terms, it is differentiated in part by its focus on the provider's intentions and the potential benefits to the recipient.

Several aspects of the interaction may be of interest, including:

- The type of support provided.
- The quantity, timing, and/or frequency of support provided.
- Whether the support was received or simply is perceived as available.
- The recipient's satisfaction with the level of support provided or available.
- The relationship between the parties involved.
- Whether or not the support has been or will be reciprocated.

The types of social support fall into five general categories. **Concrete support** refers to tangible items, such as financial assistance, goods, or services. For example, a recovering mom may receive rides to outpatient treatment. **Emotional support** includes provision of love, caring, sympathy, and other positive feelings. **Advice support** refers to helpful advice, information, and suggestions. For example, a senior may ask a friend's opinion regarding which doctor to see. **Companionship support** refers to the presence of others with whom to participate in meaningful or enjoyable activities. Companionship is considered to provide the individual with a sense of belonging to a group.

Differentiating among the intangible types of support (emotional, appraisal, informational, and companionship) can be difficult, as can quantifying the level of support provided. Collection of information typically is limited to whether or not the specific type of support was provided during the specified time period and, perhaps, the frequency with which the support was provided.

Some researchers have suggested that the quantity of support received is less important to well-being than the individual's perception that support is available if needed. This distinction between received and perceived support has proven valuable in clarifying how social relations influence well-being. Received support appears to be more important in the face of specific problems or stressors, whereas perceived support seems to be of ongoing benefit. Measures of perceived support include questions regarding whether the resident has someone in whom to confide, someone to provide emotional support, or someone to provide tangible support should the need arise.

1.2 Application Example

Karen is a 36-year-old Caucasian woman who is divorced and referred to treatment due to her recent DUI on the way home from her 8-year-old son's soccer practice with him in the car. Karen is a child of an alcoholic father who died of his alcoholism, and this is her second treatment episode. She completed an outpatient treatment program five years ago, did not follow-through with a referral to Alcoholics Anonymous, and started drinking again during her divorce two years ago. Karen scored a 4 on the ACEs assessment and has been treated for clinical depression with a history of nerve pain in her legs. She is in an Action Stage of Change due to custody fears, and indicates she is an 8 on the Readiness to Change Ruler.

She has Anxious Attachment strategies that she numbs with alcohol, acknowledging that she is easily triggered emotionally. This has been particularly true since the divorce, where her depression and anxiety have exacerbated. She is beginning to see that she has been sharing too much emotionally with her son, Alex, so has found the emotional regulation skills she is learning helpful. Karen has identified that she does not "read" people very well because she has always avoided feedback from others; she does not see herself and her impact on others accurately. In fact, most of her friends are other drinkers at the wine bar where she drinks regularly. Her counselor, Juan, discovered on her RFQ that she tends toward hypermentalizing, and Karen does have a tendency to tell long-winded stories that do not always seem to have a point, even though she feels very strongly about what she is sharing.

In treatment she learned that she has RBF, which she found hilarious, so it began to make sense for her that her husband always thought she was angry at him when she wasn't feeling anything at all. In fact, she has felt "numb" most of the time for most of her life.

Karen is meeting with her counselor, Juan, to review her connections with others in the outside community.

"So, Karen, when we looked at your MIRC during the ASAM assessment, it looks that you don't feel like you have a lot of people in your world that see you as successful, and then you don't necessarily feel people have your back. Does that sound right to you?"

Karen nods. *"I guess I'm not surprised."*

"How much of feeling this way is connected to your alcoholism versus feeling like this for a longer period of time in your life?"

"I never thought about it, but I think I've felt this way a long time, but my drinking and DUI has made it worse. People in my life are so disappointed in me, and I feel like such a loser. It makes it worse that my ex-husband is probably laughing at me because I relapsed . . . now he has a chance to take Alex like he wanted to do all along. Maybe he should – I really blew it. The only people I feel have my back are my mom and bar friends, and they're probably drunks like me!" Karen exclaims.

"It sounds like you recognize that as much as you enjoy your bar friends, you get that they may not be the most stable support group in the long run."

"Yeah, but they don't judge me. Not like my sister, who's always rolling her eyes at me. She's so perfect!"

"What do you mean by "perfect?"

"You know, she never gets in trouble, isn't divorced, has perfect children, never been arrested."

"She's made different choices, Karen; she's not a superior person."

"Yeah, well tell her and my ex-husband, Bob!"

"It sounds like you feel like they gang up on you?"

"I think my sister thinks my ex-husband is a better parent and Alex SHOULD be living with him full-time. Like I am a bad influence on him. She says I'm just like my drunk father."

"From what you've told me, your dad never tried to stop drinking, and you have successfully been sober once before. There's something about you and your willingness to change that might be very different from your dad."

"I never thought about it that way. Now that you say that, when I was listening to Sarah in group yesterday and she was talking about her alcoholic dad, I could SEE how she was different. Do you think people can see that in me?"

"I suspect they can. How would you feel about asking for feedback from the group later today? Would you trust their feedback?"

"Some of them."

"What we are going to work on is creating a Social Network Map for you to figure out who can play what role in your life as you enter a sober lifestyle after residential treatment. This is key, because we know from the research that people who feel connected have a much better shot at staying sober than people who try and do it alone. They wind up going back for support to places that supported their using. Does that make sense?"

"Like, I would start going back to the bar to see my friends because I was lonely?"

"Exactly. So, we need to get a sense of who is in your life and what relationships you have that can be strengthened to help you feel like you have a community. Plus, you'll continue to have your Peer counselor, Ashley, meeting with you for the rest of the year to bounce things off of and even go to meetings with you for support."

Chapter Two

Developing a Social Network Map

The social network map collects information on the total size and composition of the network, the extent to which network members provide various types of support, and the nature of the relationships as perceived by the person completing the map. Administering the map involves listing network members in each of seven domains: (1) household (people with whom you live); (2) family/relatives; (3) friends; (4) people from work or school; (5) people from recovery support groups (i.e. Twelve Steps), clubs, or church; (6) neighbors and; (7) agencies and formal service providers.[123]

Names and or initials of network members are visually displayed on the network map. After the composition of the network has been identified, a series of questions are asked regarding the nature of network relationships. These questions concern the types of support available (emotional, informational, concrete), the extent to which network members are critical of the individual, direction (Is the direction of help reciprocal or in one direction?), the closeness of relationships, frequency of contacts (Are they stable?), and length of relationships. Responses are recorded on the map.

2.1 Administration

Step One: Directions: Developing a Social Network Map

Let's take a look at who is in your social network by putting together a social network map. (show map). We can use first names or initials because I am not that interested in knowing particular people and I will not be contacting the people we talk about without your consent.

Think back to these past few months, especially since treatment began. What people have been important to you? They may have been people you saw, talked with, or wrote letters to. This includes people who made you feel good, people who made you feel bad, and others who just played a part in your life. They may be people who have an influence on the way you make decisions during this time.

There is no right or wrong number of people identified on your map. Right now, just list as many people as you can think of to list on the sheet. Do you want me to write, or do you want to do the writing?

1. *First, think of the people in your household – who does that include?*

2. *Now, go around the map. What other family members would you include?*

3. *How about people from work or school?*

4. *How about people from recovery support groups (i.e. Twelve Steps), clubs, or church – whom should we include here?*

5. *What other friends haven't been listed in these other categories?*

6. *Neighbors – local shopkeepers can be included here.*

7. *Finally, list professional people or people from agencies who are involved in your life.*

8. *Look over this list. Are these people you would have considered in your social network over the last few months? (Add or delete names as needed)*

Step Two: Completing the Social Network Map

If more than 15 people are listed in the network, have them choose the "top" fifteen and then ask the questions about only those network members. Write their names on index cards.

Now I'd like to learn more about the people in your network. I'm going to write their names on the network grid in the right category, and then ask a few questions about the ways in which they help you. These are the questions I'll be asking (show them the questions), and we'll check off the names on the grid as we go through each question.

The first three questions have to do with the type of support people give you.

1. *Who would be available to help you out in **concrete** ways. For example, who would give you a ride if you needed one or store your things if you were in jail or in treatment? Divide your cards into three piles. Those who you can hardly ever rely on for concrete help, those you can rely on sometimes, and those you would almost always rely on for this type of help.*

2. *Now who would be available to offer you **emotional** support – for example to comfort you if you were upset, to be right there with you in a stressful situation, or talk about your feelings? Again, divide them into three piles. Those who you can hardly ever rely*

on for emotional support, those you can rely on sometimes, and those you would almost always rely on for this type of help.

3. Now, who would you rely on for **advice** – for example who would give you information on how to do something, help you make a big decision, or teach you something? Divide it into three piles – hardly ever, sometimes, and almost always – for this type of support. Look through your cards and select those, if any, that you feel are **critical** (either critical of you, your parenting or your lifestyle). When I say critical, I mean something that makes you feel bad or inadequate. Divide the cards into three piles – those who are hardly ever critical of you, sometimes critical of you, and almost always critical of you.

4. Now look over your cards at the **direction** of help. Divide your cards into three piles. Those people with whom help goes both ways (you help them as much as they help you), those you help more, and those who help you more.

5. Now think about how **close** you are to the people in your network. Divide the cards into three piles- those you are not very close to, those you are sort of close to, and those you are very close to.

Finally, just a few questions about **how often** you see people and **how long** you have known people in your network. Divide the names into people you just see a few times a year, people you see monthly, people you see weekly, and people you see daily. (If you see someone twice or more than twice a week put them as "daily".)

Now, divide the names into those people you have known less than a year, between 1 to 5 years, and more than 5 years. Of the people in these areas – who are the people you are sure will support your recovery, who might support you, and those who either won't support or will feel uncomfortable with your recovery.[124]

Table 5: Karen: Recording the Social Network Map

Names	1. Household 2. Family 3. Work/school 4. Support groups 5. Other friends 6. Neighbors 7. Professionals 8. Others	Concrete Support 1. Hardly ever 2. Sometimes 3. Almost always	Emotional Support 1. Hardly ever 2. Sometimes 3. Almost always	Inform./ Advice 1. Hardly ever 2. Sometimes 3. Almost always	Critical 1. Hardly ever 2. Sometimes 3. Almost always	Direction of Help 1. Goes both ways 2. You to Them 3. Them to You	Closeness 1. Hardly ever 2. Sometimes 3. Almost always	Often Seen 0. Never 1. Few times a year 2. Monthly 3. Weekly 4. Daily	Time Known 1. Less than a yr 2. 1-5 yr 3. More than 5 years
Mom	1, 2	3	2	3	2	3	2	4	3
Ex Hus	8	1	1	2	3	2	1	3	3
Alex (8 yr)	1, 2	1	3	2	2	1	3	4	3
Sister	2	1	1	1	3	none	1	1	3
Boss	3	1	2	2	2	1	2	4	3
Former Sponsor	4	2	3	2	1	3	2	3	2
Neighbor	6, 5	2	3	2	1	1	2	3	2
Psychiat	7	1	2	2	1	3	2	2	2
Bar friends	5	1	3	2	1	1	2	3	3
2 Sober friends	4	2	2	2	2	1	2	2	2
Peer counselor	7, 5	3	3	3	3	3	2	4	1
Counselor	7	2	3	2	1	3	2	4	1

APPLICATION EXAMPLE: KAREN

"It looks like we have a pretty complete overview of the people in your life, Karen" Juan observes. "Is there anyone we've missed?"

Karen studies the chart. *"It looks like my neighbor, son, bar friends, and mom are my strongest emotional support, and my former sponsor WAS a huge support before I relapsed and I stopped calling her. My mom and peer counselor are advice givers, and I do feel pretty connected to my boss. I feel guilty about taking this time off, because I know he needs me."*

"What's going on with your psychiatrist – you're only partially close to her?"

"I haven't been as honest with her about how much I've been drinking. I was afraid she would kick me out or stop giving me my meds."

"As we talk about it, do you think that would really happen?"

"Probably not."

"I am concerned at how much of your support system your son seems to be. You'll need to develop more adult friendships so he can focus more on his own life. How do you think he got to be such large support for you?"

"I don't know. I guess it's just the two of us since the divorce, and so we just talk to each other about everything. Shouldn't I be talking to him about his life?"

"Absolutely! You're doing a great job. The concern is how much YOU are sharing about your life, particularly how you feel about his dad. It puts him in a tough loyalty situation."

"My mom used to talk to me about my dad. It made us closer."

"I can see why you would think that. But looking back on it, as an adult, do you remember being worried about things your mom was worried about like your dad's drinking or the bills?"

Karen nods. *"I think it made her feel better because we were together. Like we were a team."*

"How did it make you feel?"

"Honestly, I think I was worried a lot. I remember biting my nails as a kid."

"I can imagine. The difficulty is that the kid can take on the worry but doesn't have the power to actually change the situation so has to just sit in the feelings and HOPE the adults do something about it. Does that make sense?"

"Do you think my son feels that way?"

"What do you think, Karen?"

Karen has tears in her eyes. *"Poor Alex. I didn't realize that I was doing the same thing my mom did."*

"Now that you know, YOU can change it even if your mom didn't know how. It looks like you have a couple of sober friends that might be open to spending more time with you."

"You mean Carla and Virginia. Yeah, they're friends from college and we see each other several times a year. I haven't been good about keeping in touch over the last year. I'm embarrassed to tell them I was

arrested – I'm such a loser."

"Karen, you use the term 'loser' for yourself a lot. Is that the way you are talk to yourself in your head?"

"Well, I AM a loser. I was arrested. I can't believe I let that happen, that I was that out of control and my son saw me in handcuffs. I keep picturing that scene over and over in my head and I keep seeing the look on his face. I'm so ashamed," Karen starts to cry.

Juan sits quietly and waits for Karen to collect herself.

"Karen, one of the reasons we have spent time learning about the way alcohol affects your brain and hijacks your ability to choose to drink is to give you a more realistic way to see what has happened to you. When your brain is hijacked by craving, the front part of the brain, the decision-making part, is no longer in charge. We make poor decisions and aren't able to think ahead. Does that sound familiar?"

"I keep thinking, 'What was I thinking?' You're saying that I WASN'T thinking. I was not making a choice to drink."

"What difference would it make to the way you think about yourself if that was true?"

"I guess it would mean that if I wasn't drinking, I would be able to choose."

"And would you choose to get in a position to get arrested in front of your son?"

Karen sits quietly. *"No. No, I wouldn't."*

"I don't think so either," Juan agrees. "Here's the other concern I have. I'm worried that you're assuming that everyone else would be as critical of you as YOU are, and so aren't using the support system you need to stay sober. When we look at this chart, where do you see opportunities to deepen your trust and attachment?"

"Hmmm. I could definitely try calling my old sponsor and see if she will start meeting with me again."

"What do you think she would say?"

"I'm not sure. She'll probably ask me where I went and why I didn't call her when I started drinking again."

Juan laughs, *"That would be a typical sponsor response! Once you told her your story, do you think she will agree to take you back on?"*

"Can you sit with me when I call her?"

"Yes, I can. We'll do that during our next session, how would that be?"

Karen nods and looks relieved.

Juan continues, *"When you look at this chart, where do you see potential triggers or impediments to your sobriety?"*

Karen furrows her brows. *"My sister and my ex. I think they want me to fail so I'll lose custody."*

"Can I ask if you've ever talked to them about your recovery?"

"I don't talk to them unless I have to."

"So, you don't actually KNOW how they might feel about your sobriety."

"I know they think I'm a loser, and irresponsible."

"Well, you don't make good choices when you drink. However, this is not who you are as a person. It's a very important distinction."

Juan continues. *"It sounds like you'll need to work with your Peer counselor to create a plan when you have to encounter your ex. Maybe you can hold off before engaging your sister. However, I want you to consider the possibility that your ex-husband might WANT you to be sober and would be willing to help you with Alex to make this happen."*

Karen looks skeptical.

"You haven't mentioned your bar friends. How do you want to handle this?"

"I feel bad about disappearing. They're probably wondering where I am."

"Probably. Have you ever seen someone else disappear from the bar?"

Karen thinks. *"Yeah, I think I have."*

"What happened?"

"Well, we talked about them for a few weeks, and then we forgot about them."

"What would it feel like to think about that happening to you?"

"Maybe they don't care as much about me as I think they do. That makes me sad."

"I can understand this. What bonded you was the alcohol, not sharing your lives. The goal is to connect to people in your life that share lots of different parts of your life." Juan continues, *"You've done a great job, Karen. This is hard. Next time we meet we'll call your sponsor, and we'll work on making a recovery village with the chart you filled out today. Before we meet, I want you to think if there is someone else you could add like someone from work, cousins, maybe even a parent of one of Alex's friends. You've been pretty emotionally unavailable yourself, so you may not have considered them as options."*

2. 2 Recovery Village

Karen has a lot to work with here, and in the discussion, it might be possible to create a pretty realistic RECOVERY support "village" with the huts indicating who, from her social network, are the most available to healthy attachments going forward.

Using colored pens, write the names or initials around the "hut." Draw a line between the people in the network who talk to each other about you.

Next to each appropriate hut have the resident list the initials and phone number for the support person.

Table 6: Karen: **Recovery Village**

Social Network Map

Date _____ 8/1/20

CONCRETE
Mom (661) 854-3078
Julia: Sponsor (661) 923-4591
Tom: Neighbor (661) 462-0194
Ashley: Peer (661-994-0254

ADVICE
Mom (661) 254-7620
Julia: (661) 923-4591
Ashley: Peer (661-994-0254

EMOTIONAL
Mom (661) 254-7620
Julia: (661) 923-4591
Carla (661) 426-7622
Virginia (661) 331-0388
Ashley: Peer (661-994-0254

DIRECTION
Mom (661) 854-3078
Tom: Neighbor (661) 462-0194
Bob: Ex (661) 221-3847
Kevin: Boss (661) 731-0284

CRITICAL
Andrea: Sister (721) 328-5549
Bob: Ex (661) 221-3847

YOU

SUPPORT
Mom (661) 254-7620
Julia: (661) 923-4591
Carla (661) 426-7622
Virginia (661) 331-0388
Ashley: Peer (661-994-0254

CLOSE
Mom (661) 254-7620
Julia: (661) 923-4591

Chapter Three

Relapse Prevention Planning

Relapse prevention planning has been taking place all along as issues have been identified. More formally, it will be time for the Peer counselor to be more involved in the aftercare planning as the resident prepares to transition to the next phase of treatment. The Peer counselor will be following the resident for the first full year of recovery, and so scheduling and calendaring will be part of the process. The resident is most likely not used to having ongoing trusted support in their attempts to maintain sobriety, though may have made cursory attempts in the past. If they have, they may believe they use social support more effectively than their relapse history would indicate. Hopefully, the social support network mapping discussion and process will have made this clearer to them.

3.1 Common Triggers of Substance Abuse Relapse Begin with Attachment Threats

Post Acute Withdrawal symptoms: anxiety, troubling thoughts and memories intruding on your sleep, irritability, mood swings, and poor sleep up to 6 months to one year of recovery. In addition, the immune system may still be struggling with vulnerability to hyper and hypo arousal. May need medical or psychiatric support.

Poor self-care: For example: poor stress management, irregular eating, sleep deprivation, skipping support group meetings, too much caffeine and nicotine making you jittery, ignoring your thoughts and appointments with professionals, allowing "sketchy" and unsafe people to spend time with you, refusing to allow structure in your life, returning to unsafe places that were part of your using lifestyle, agreeing to sex when you don't want to have sex because you feel "obligated", not trusting others will be available for you, withholding from trustworthy people).

Relationships: For example: paranoia about people's motives and feelings about you, disbelieving others when they say they care about you, distrusting people's intentions, lying about your intentions and withholding information from your social support, using sex to manipulate relationships, not clarifying communication confusion and allowing relational breakages and distancing and attachment disruption. Returning to denial that you need other people in your recovery to be successful – you can "do this" by yourself. Blaming others for making you uncomfortable and "making you" want to use. This creates an opening for a return to attachment to substances.

Defensive behaviors: For example: dishonesty about emotions and behaviors, irritable and harsh language toward others, being quick to take offense, "testing" people's attachment to you, using walls like silence, isolation or anger to be distant, denying that people matter to you, telling yourself that YOU don't matter, not setting boundaries to "keep" people connected to you, refusing to be accountable for your behaviors, attempting to manipulate and control others because you think they are pulling away from you, over-reacting with agitation or shutting down in even small situations, withholding sex as a power and control strategy, taking yourself way too seriously, turning even small situations into a crisis to make sure you are cared about.

Cognitive Distortions: For example: a return to denial about severity of addiction or alcoholism, misreading other people more frequently, misinterpreting others' intentions and motivations, returning to a self-referential perspective where everything is about you, withholding empathy and affection because you decide someone doesn't "deserve" it, harshly judging others, refusal to learn new information, feeling threatened and panicky when given new information so can't think, no longer reflecting on your own thoughts and motivations and no longer able to be curious about the thoughts of others, **cognitive rigidity** – my way is the only way to think. No longer able to see yourself with perspective.

A good plan will include:

- Identification of specific triggers, **especially attachment threats**
- Tools and methods for coping with stress and triggers
- Healthy lifestyle strategies and self-improvement ideas
- A maintenance plan for daily life
- Communication ideas for family and loved ones
- **Repair strategies** when relationship ruptures happen
- Accountability methods
- Goals

A relapse prevention plan will feature trusted attachment people, a concrete course of action, outlining coping mechanisms and ideas for managing cravings and triggers in times of stress.   Returning to the Readiness Ruler will be helpful at this juncture, and you will use it for each item of the plan to evaluate both their willingness and the realism of the items on their plan. It is better to have a less robust but more genuine plan.

Chapter Four

Scheduling a Support System Review of the Relapse Prevention Plan with the Resident

Over the course of the treatment and the development of a social support network map, we have developed a strong sense of the people the resident is willing to include in their recovery process. It will be important to schedule a meeting with the group, including the sponsor and outside therapist if the resident has identified one. Also included will be the Peer counselor who will follow the resident so that the family will be familiar with them and their role with the resident. Confidentiality will still be enforced even in the next phase of treatment, *so the support system needs to be notified of the limits of communication between the Peer counselor and the support system.* This may include the Peer counselor being willing to receive information about the resident or the family member when the family is concerned, while not revealing information the resident has disclosed. This includes always informing the resident that the family has called, and the general gist of the call. The resident will be referred to the family member for more details.

The primary concern is not becoming a secret-keeper, but that communication is transparent with limited detailed information. For example, if a family member calls with a concern that the resident has returned to substance use, it will be important to address this with the resident as the very next meeting, including the fact that the family member has called. We are all on the same team, which is a concept that will need to be reinforced with attachment disrupted clients repeatedly, especially the more paranoid avoidants!

When meeting with the support system, it will be helpful to review the components of the plan and identify the steps the support people are willing to take to be a trusted and responsive support person. Al-anon should be HIGHLY recommended, and the support system should be provided with basic information about attachment styles, the definition of addiction, and the neurology of addiction. It is an ideal time to provide information, address myths and concerns the support system may have about the addiction process and **clarify everyone's boundaries and expectations of each other.**

Make sure the resident has a copy of their plan and make a copy for anyone that the resident is willing to have a copy to assist the client to stay on track.

4.1 Program Completion

As the three phases draw to an end, it will be time to have the resident take the attachment evaluation again, the RFQ again, and complete Readiness Ruler identifying their stage of change, and complete the program exit evaluation.

Ending relationships peacefully is not a skill most of our residents have, and they will need support to transition without a return to old defensive avoidance or anxious, or disorganized strategies. It would be normal to expect an increase in symptoms and predict this will be a powerful intervention.

Take the time to review their **Attachment assessment** with them again, and review the progress they have made, as well as common strategies they have used and identified through the treatment episode.

Take the time to review their **Emotional Regulation Strategies** and see if there needs to be an adjustment.

Take the time to review their **RFQ** with them, commenting on the progress they have made in their ability to self-reflect, and identifying signs that they are using hypomentalizing or hypermentalizing strategies to avoid self-reflection because they have been triggered and their arousal system has jumped up.

Finally, review their **Social Support Network Map** and **Recovery Village** with them one last time to see if there needs to be adjustments and that all necessary phone numbers have been added.

Complete the Program ASAM discharge plan to make sure all six dimensions have been addressed and prepare the logistics of the transition. (Who is picking them up? Make sure they have a written schedule for the next month, and an appointment is on the books with the Peer Counselor, etc.).

Chapter Five

What if I am an Individual Practitioner or Operate an IOP?

I have given this a great deal of thought. It was my bias that early addiction treatment is done most effectively in a residential setting, though it could be that depending on the avoidant attachment structure of the client, the Individual Practitioner model may be the only practical model. The clients will not agree to participate in a group milieu, though often possess an Action Stage of Change mentality. It turns out my bias was misplaced, and once I opened my Attachment Infused Addiction Treatment® Outpatient model, I discovered that Intensive Outpatient worked very well!

My heart always draws me to people who have returned to substances after sobriety many times, the "multiple-relapsing client." As I discussed earlier in the text, it is my observation that interrupted attachment styles, and the subsequent trauma that underlie these sobriety struggles, leads to a belief that, "Vodka makes more sense than people." I decided to meet the clients where they were willing to meet me, which was in my office!

A Caveat About Harm Reduction

The AIAT® model is most effective for people who were in Preparation/Action Stages of Change. Knowing this, I did agree to use this model with several people who requested Harm Reduction initially. They wanted to reduce their alcohol use though, not abstain completely, and were highly motivated. And, for the first six months of the structured program they did, in fact, reduce their drinking levels. They reported they were HIGHLY satisfied, and had begun to implement some of the attachment strategies changes we had learned. Their primary relationships were going more smoothly, and they felt more confidence and energy. One of my clients reconnected with an estranged parent, developed hobbies, started developing a friend group, and he found a boyfriend! The boyfriend was a drinker...

I, however, did NOT feel highly satisfied, because I could see they still believed they could control their use, and had not implemented the group support I offered. They had done a lot of reading, tried to use tracking apps... they were committed to thinking their way to sobriety. In all honesty, I felt sad because I KNOW this is a medical disease, which we had reviewed together, and they all had extensive family history of substance use.

As most of my clients chose to do, they continued in weekly therapy with me and within a few months began to have what they called "bad nights," when they were unable to control their drinking. They had switched to beer, so were not drinking "hard" liquor, and there were fewer of these. However, the "bad nights" usually included bourbon or whiskey, and I could see that the incidents they reported were only going to get more frequent. They began to address the stressors of their relationships - their primary trigger- and I have integrated their significant others into the treatment plan to support the reality of their continued unavailability when they drink, even if it is 50% less, as one person said.

Sample Treatment Plan for Harm Reduction

Client: H.K.

Stated or Identified Motivation for Treatment (What is the most important thing the clients wants you to help them with?)

He has been considering the impact of his alcohol use after the birth of his son.

Current Placement Dimension Rating (See Dimensions below 1- 6) Stage of Change: Preparation

Dim 1 Action (1) No current withdrawal - reports experiencing night sweats after first 24 hours sober, last one two days ago. Connects this to bourbon. Not interested in complete abstinence at this time. Drinking daily, would like to drink less frequently. If explores abstinence, need to discuss MAT.

Dim 2 Action (0) 300 mg Gabapentin 1x a night for shoulder nerves. Blood pressure higher when drinking, and cholesterol need to be monitored, Dropped 10- 15 pounds last 6 months.

Dim 3 Prep (2) No current craving and distress stated while exploring early attachment interruption on current relationship strategies, including use of alcohol. Increased threat assessment due to early trauma, including hypervigilance. When drinking more heavily reports ongoing irritability, fatigue, increased cognitive rigidity.

Dim 4 Action   (0) Is exploring role of alcohol and its impact on parenting, work, marriage, self-identity. Is fully engaged.

Dim 5 Cont.   (3) Not completely clear about triggers, though exploring early childhood triggers adult relationships at work and marriage

Dim 6 Action   (0)Home and work is stable and lives with wife and son.

II. What problem(s) with High and Medium severity rating are of greatest concern at this time?

ASAM 3

Problem: Lapses into cognitive rigidity and distancing when triggered in primary relationships

Goal: Patient will recognize triggers using body cues and internal dialogue to interrupt rigidity, practice mentalizing and co-regulating with wife when reactivity has diminished.

Action

- Utilize hypervigilance toward body cues and shifts to increase ability to recognize changes in physical stance and vocal tone
- Attend to internal dialogue and use CBT challenge statements to level reactive distance planning
- Utilize strategies to lower reactivity and repair strategies when relationship is ruptured.

ASAM 5

Problem: Ambivalent about sobriety as the role of alcohol is not fully clear, and exploring **moderate use patterns** to retain the presence of alcohol in his life.

Goal: Patient will identify the advantages and disadvantages of use pattern and its impact on achieving the quality of life he seeks.

Action:

- Explore past and current impact of substance use as he returns to use, noticing increasing use patterns as they arise.
- Continue to complete curriculum assessments and weighing costs and benefits to ongoing use of alcohol.

I discontinued offering my model for harm reduction for new clients FOR ME, not them. It is very possible more harm reduction people would come, but I have been an addiction counselor for too long, and so I honestly feel I am enabling the drinking even if the client feels they are making progress. YOU may make a different calculation, and I hope so, in a way, because I know the clients feel it is valuable.

What Has Worked in My Program

It is my experience that the individual/IOP version of Attachment Infused Addiction Treatment (AIAT)® has been more effective with people who are committed to sobriety, have already achieved sobriety through treatment and are transferring to me for IOP, or have relapsed and are struggling to maintain or grow in their recovery due to the attachment struggles we have explored so far. They may still be struggling with consistent sobriety, or they will find themselves substituting over-work, codependent behaviors, or food in lieu of alcohol and drugs because they are unable to use the support available to them in their lives. In fact, I addressed this model originally for Codependents in *Awakening Hope: A Developmental, Biological, Behavioral Approach to Codependency Recovery.* My premise in the text is that many, many addicts were codependent due to early attachment disruption prior to discovering addictive substances, and once sober, will engage in codependent strategies in their relationships.

If you were going to apply the AIAT® model to a person with current addictive behavioral or substance use, it would be important to assess the level of care they need and refer clients to substance abuse treatment who might require detoxification. Outpatient detoxification is an option in some cases; however, they will possibly be physically compromised and could benefit from medical detoxification and craving management, something far outside the licensed therapist's scope of practice if you are operating in an individual practice and not a clinic. It is possible they have a cooccurring disorder, which may mean you can continue to see the client for mental health support during their treatment episode to maintain your alliance, which would be strongly indicated in an attachment model like AIAT®. A return to use frequently happens in this model, and I will address this in a few pages. We measure time by a calendar, not "all or nothing," so using for two days is an improvement from 6 days. However, the goal is still going to be abstinence in order to support a shift to relational versus substance use soothing.

A. Overview of Goal of Treatment

A QUICK REVIEW:

In these early days we are engaging the resident through genuine attention to their neurological and emotional state. *The specific goal for hyperactivated patients is to reduce their need for reassurance from others and "talk themselves off the cliff"; and for the deactivated patient, the goal is to reduce their tendency to cut off emotional experience.* This will allow the client to engage people in their ongoing recovery and emotional regulation in lieu of a substance. To create the foundation for this, we need to offer a role as a secure base for ongoing treatment engagement. This more structured version of this model is six months; however, it is my clinical experience that clients remain in ongoing individual and/or group counseling for several years. I recognize this is challenging in a CalAIMS/MediCal environment, and so program development will require you to develop staffing and case management structure that allows for an ongoing model.

How do we accomplish engagement?

Another quick review: Wallin[125], says that secure base is promoted by collaborative communication, which involves four elements:

1. Fostering a collaborative dialogue that is inclusive of all domains of experience.

2. Actively identifying ongoing ruptures and fostering repair.

3. Upgrading the dialogue and the mentalizing to "higher levels of awareness".

    • Translating the mentalization of early attachment into psychotherapy into developing *metacognitive (reflecting on one's own thoughts and thoughts of others) skill* is a process of joint awareness in which the client's mental states are the object of attention.

    • The three ways to develop metacognitive skills are: **validation, therapist self-disclosure pertaining to mental states, and therapist sharing of experiences pertaining to mental states.**[93]

4. Providing a real relationship to which therapists and patient alike struggle with and fully engaging with each other. We provide a corrective experience.

As we move forward in this section of the text, I will operationalize these further, in addition to the application examples I have already provided.

Here is an example:

Client goes dark for *five* days: not responding to OMD nurse or the counselor.

When he does, *"I'm high and haven't been home. I'm at work right now and hella busy. But yes, for the most part I'm okay."*

Counselor texts, *"Hi, R., I hope you will still come tomorrow. Remember the goal is to get stable ASAP. **Thinking about you.** "*

Client, *"I'll be there. "*

He did, in fact, attend his session the next day. The counselor was able to communicate that the client matters to her, and she would notice if he did not attend the session. The point is to offer a secure base to see and hear the client accurately. More about continued use in a few pages.

B. Orientation

If you assess the client can manage their substance abuse fairly effectively, you may decide to proceed with the Attachment Infused Addiction Treatment® model individually in an IOP format. You will need to orient them to the model, which includes introducing them to the role of psychoeducation. Formal psychoeducation is not typically part of individual counseling, so the client may be unfamiliar with this approach. As in most first therapy sessions, we are largely building rapport and creating as safe a connection as they will allow.

Before leaving their first session, we will ask them to agree to the medical assessment, and if it becomes obvious that they need immediate psychiatric medication review or craving management, we ask them to agree to this as well. We are indicating here that we are taking their body seriously - addiction is a medical illness. As we move forward, we will address sleep hygiene, nutritional support, and a physical movement plan. Physical recovery is imperative for recovering addicts.

I ask them to watch or watch with them. Everything YOU think you know about addiction is wrong | Johann Hari I TED (Youtube.com)

Orientation to the Model Sample:

"Hi John, I wanted to give you an overview of the way I address addiction treatment, because it might be different from the approaches you have tried before. I believe that when we were young, some of us did not have a consistent and safe adult to rely upon to help us manage our emotional world, and we learned to soothe ourselves with substances instead of people. Over time, the substance or behavior we used to manage our early feelings hijacks our neurological system and we become addicted. Using is no longer a choice at that point, we need the drug or alcohol or feel "normal." When we try to quit, our internal distress gets so intense that we return to our drug use. If this is true, you may have tried to stay sober in programs like Alcoholic Anonymous and found yourself unable to connect with the others in the room even though they were open to connecting with you.

In the model I am going to use, The Attachment Infused Addiction Treatment® model, and the goal is to help you learn to engage with people effectively when in distress rather than using substances. Connect with people instead of vodka! We are going to use psycho-educational material to help you learn more about your brain and how substances and emotional stress have impacted your body. In fact, I am going to ask you to get a physical and blood panel that includes a request that your doctor take a look at your adrenal system, since that is highly impacted by relationship and addiction lifestyle stress. We need to treat any physical issues that may have developed, and consider mental health or craving medication if necessary, if you are not already taking it. We don't want to ask you to participate in treatment if you have physical issues we don't know about!

We are going to use assessment tools for you to learn more about you, and ways that you struggle to feel connected and attached to other people, and the behaviors you might do that get in your way in relationships. We are going to look at your social support system and figure out who is available for what type of support in your world, and how to grow that support to help you stay in long-term recovery.

We are going to practice some of the skills you need to use in your relationships in our relationship, and I will be giving you feedback about what I see, your patterns, and how you affect me when things come up. My goal is to be as transparent as I can with you and invite you to do the same. Ultimately, I will be asking you to practice what we are doing *in the outside world. This may mean joining a small support group at some point to create a larger practice lab!*

A NOTE ABOUT GROUP

This population are often non-joiners so you will not ask this of them for the first month. The majority of my clients resisted this, and I would end up forming small groups (four clients) of avoidant-style clients who were willing to attend because I was in individual therapy with them. It was part of OUR attachment that they were willing to try, even if skeptical. Because of the nature of the group, and our history with psychoeducation the structure of our time together was consistent:

- Open with a short check in
- Introduce the Psychoeducation topic and begin discussion
- Open Sharing
- Close with 15 minutes of SSP to practice co-regulating

I always had a worksheet with a different topic each week to discuss, which allowed them to avoid the "small talk" they were afraid of initially, and established points of similarity. I was surprised and tickled at how much laughing we did, as they spoke about their internal thoughts about other "needy" people and recognized their own over reactivity and under reactivity. They supported each other when we would take risks in the "real world" to be emotionally honest or vulnerable. Over time the open sharing portion became longer, and we wound up adding 15 minutes to the length of the group, so we had enough time! I have a group that has continued for over two years, at this point. We initially moved to every other week after a year and are now shifting into a periodic workshop format. One of the members has also added AA, but will only do "Rat Bastards," a men's 14-week group where they have a structured approach to working the steps. He feels safer with the structured, predictable response and sharing with the same group at his table every week. I have another person who simply will not do any other option but does not miss our little group!

Opening with Psychoeducation each week is important. I can tell you that I would pick my topic based on what I was hearing during the week and see a common topic. I would put the topic in google search and find an article I could crib for the psychoeducation piece.

Here is a partial list of some of the topics I have covered:

- 12 Steps to Getting real emotional Honesty
- 5 Ingredients for Repair
- Identifying an Avoidant Attachment Style
- Am I Distress Intolerant?
- 10 Signs Fear is Running Your Life
- Authentic Communication and 10 Ways to Achieve It
- Knowling When To Speak Up
- The Cognitive Control and Flexibility Questionnaire
- Four Tips for Adults with Avoidant Attachment to Self-Regulate in a Healthy Way
- Humor Styles Questionnaire
- How To Socialize
- 6 Tips to Maintain Lasting and Meaningful Relationships

It was common that we wound up taking more than one session to cover the topic due to the length of sharing, which was obviously more valuable. Psychoeducation created a safe and predictable outline, a jumping off point designed to embed and operationalize the attach-ment style strategies we were learning as part of the AIAT® program.

When I asked them about the benefits of group, especially in understanding how their avoidant style manifests in the world, they mentioned,

"Understand the intensity and impact of other's energy and ways they may create distance, like abruptness or hostility, shutting down, saying something shocking. . . "

"Less judgmental of myself and others," as other people's response made more sense to them, and they could take the behavior of others' less personally.

"Relationships include obligation." We spent a fair amount of time on this as relationships are not entered into lightly, they will then be perceived as a "ride or die" level of commitment. This helps explain some of the hesitance of entering new relationships, because there is the automatic thought, *"What are they going to want from me? What*

is this going to take," versus seeing other people entering their world as opportunities, or curiosity, or chances to explore and expand. It is as though their availability is in such short supply that new relationships need to be weighed very carefully.

"*I am more self-accepting,*" was common feedback. Prior to meeting others, most of the group had honestly believed they were the ONLY ones who responded in the world the way they did. This makes sense, as they so seldom share their internal experience, they would not have had a chance to "reality test" with others and normalize choices like; ALWAYS taking their own car, or wearing headphones to avoid conversation, or wanting to leave the room when they encountered group energy of any kind so frequently hiding in the bathroom during events!

"*Things that I do, like vilifying people who make me uncomfortable, now make sense to me.*" This relates to the psychoeducation component and developing vocabulary for how we are perceived by others as well as how we organize our thoughts about others.

At the end of the day, what makes the opportunity for avoidantly attached folks to share experience so precious is how rare it is for them, and how reassuring it is to find the same people annoying and laugh at their avoidant internal voice that they so seldom express externally.

Structure of the Program

Once you have oriented the client to model, you schedule to see them twice a week individually, and if using the OMD tracking, get them their monitoring equipment. The first session the following week will be psychoeducation, and you give them their first module and binder with a new module each successive week, and the next session will be individual counseling. You will follow this pattern and then add either a support group or a small group of your own so they will be attending three times a week for the remainder of the 90-day section of the program. After 90 days, the client will return the OMD equipment, and they will shift to once a week PLUS group and do these for the next 90 days. You can increase the frequency as needed.

A NOTE ABOUT OMD

OverSightMD™ is a tool I offer in my program to help clients develop the skills to learn to read their physical responses to their emotions. As avoidant people have often learned to down-regulate, they wander around in the world separated from their bodies and are missing valuable cues about their internal and external experiences. The OversightMD™ dashboard offers a biomedical tool (actual monitoring stickers on your body that provide "real-time" data to a nurse and case management team who can reach out when they see physical changes that often indicate vulnerability to an impending relapse. It is connected to an app on the client's phone and includes a daily log and readiness to change score that you see in the treatment plans above. The OMD nurse will reach out to me and the client when they notice significant shifts in the client's data to try and connect them with what was happening when their body was shifting.

I found this equipment MOST effective for anxiously attached clients because they will more likely utilize the support of the nurse as part of the team. The avoidant clients were compliant and were primarily interested in their sleeping patterns being monitored. This was valuable, as people in early recovery have disrupted sleep patterns, so they utilized the monitoring more for this than recognizing emotional shifts. I learned it was better to introduce this equipment further into the treatment program, like the second 90-day section, because their bodies are more stabilized so shifts can be more easily connected to internal cues.

The other option with more motivated clients is to have them use tracker apps on their phones or fit bits. The point is to learn to recognize your physical cues. The OMD is also especially helpful for anxiously attached clients because the nurse becomes part of your co-regulating team with client. This is very valuable is you work in private practice alone.

The OMD equipment is not helpful for harm reduction clients as they are still using substances.

Here is a sample of how the OMD sticker helps when it works:

Week One Notes:

Between first and second session the client had used. Was in McDonald's for lunch when an old celli was in the line behind him. They hugged and sat down to have lunch. The celli went to the rest room, and when he came back slid a paper towel covering meth across the table and offered to use together. So they did.

WINS:

Contacted OMD, RPMsticker nurse monitor:

"Thank you for checking up on me because at times I feel I don't deserve to have people who care about me, but the fact you're checking up on me now shows that I do matter and that this does matter, so thank you."

He told his girlfriend about his use and didn't disappear and went to work the next day. When high, sat in car the whole time and was miserable. However, no new crime. **Came to treatment anyway**.

He acknowledges he needs psych medication to manage his emotional regulation - anxiety too much and overrides his impulse control. Gave him the 800 number to call for the county for an appointment for behavioral health. He will use his MediCal or may have Kaiser. Still denies "craving."

Note: later in treatment he revealed that he never wants to admit craving because that would make him a "typical' addict and he couldn't blame it on stress.

Week Two

Used in the AM. Didn't call his counselor because it was such a "small amount" = minimized it. Got secretive. Got through the day, then used again and couldn't sleep, felt paranoid, slept on the couch. Went to friend's house to sleep. Hadn't slept well in two days. Flushed the rest at friend's house, took a shower, and came to see the counselor.

As he was using, the OMD nurse had noticed the fluctuations in his readings, and she was able to speak to him at length about his craving to use. He said it was the first time he had ever talked about using WHILE using, and laughingly suggested that we were *"fucking up his high."*

"This relapse/get sober repeat cycle is harder than just staying in my addiction."

The counselor pointed out that, *" Normally you will use for 45 days. You are using 3 days a week for the last three weeks – that's nine days. We are going in the right direction."*

Note: realizes his cannot be a functional addict – "losing my best friend" or PRIMARY ATTACHMENT

Second session of Week 2

Pt presents as tearful, anxious that people around him can see he is impaired. Storing drugs at work.

Client states, *"You are the only reason I haven't fallen further into my disease. You and [OMD nurse] always seem to message me when I need it – non-judgmental."*

Plan:

- Add an additional RPMsticker in car for better real-time data
- Will stay with friend that night, but check in with girlfriend and provide location
- Return to counseling this week
- Activate gym membership provided by the counselor to have a safe place to be other than his car.
- CALL KAISER

Has never talked to treatment professionals while using before – states. *"You remind me of how a mom can be without the craziness"*. His mom: *"You have to help yourself: You got yourself here."*

States that [OMD nurse] and the counselor pull him out of his self-pity.

Week Ten

[OMD nurse] called client noting shifts in his body temperature and heartrate. His baseline is beginning to develop since he has stopped using. Is going to meet with kid's bio-dad today to ask about moving in January, so is anxious.

Notices that adversity is like growth mindset and is resilience building.

RESILIENCE QUIZ score: 61 – moderate.

Realizes he can't multi-task, and not sure if this is drug related or the way he works.

He is taking Clonidine and vitamins to sleep and better rested.

Offered that he has more awareness of stressors and reactions when wearing biosticker. Noticing even when he is not wearing it because it has become a habit to pay attention to his physical reactions.

Continued Use

You will notice in this sample exchange that the AIAT® approach is to expect a return to use, and continue treatment both via text and continuing session schedule. The goal is to stabilize within 24 hours, and talk about the use without shame, but with curiosity. Having a plan creates more agency and engagement. The OMD sticker indicates physical symptoms, so we have the data in real time. Remember, I designed this for people with multiple relapse histories—the "feral" ones, so intense structure will trigger failure for them.

For example:

Recognized urge to use over the weekend and was able to detail it. Primary reason didn't use was girlfriend and wanting to prove he could make it longer than a week.

Relapse Sequence:

Sat: Woke up tired, slept to 10 instead of 7. Pissed off about sleeping later. Tired of being tired. Thinks, *"I know how to fix that."* Then started to think about getting high 11-2 pm. Instead went on errands with girlfriend to stay supervised. Decided to do mushrooms with girlfriend instead of meth, so picked up shrooms and dinner and went home. Sunday woke up at 11, started cleaning house, playing video games, dinner. *"Buddy system works for me."*

SUCCESS: *Always thought stress triggers his using. Now sees he was NOT stressed, but he was* coming out of his skin, restless -CRAVINGS. Wanted to believe he was stronger than his biology-" but I have been lying to myself about that. I call it stress. If I have cravings, it means I am not unique - I am an addict just like everyone else."

This is a "high touch" model, meaning the team (the nurse and counselor) are highly available via text, so this is not a 9 to 5 model. Most of my clients are avoidant, and rarely contact me, but the anxiously attached clients do. The nurse and I would normally initiate the check ins with the avoidants. It was a sign of progress when they DID contact us, but it was rare. When they do contact me it is about scheduling or occasionally send me a meme.

For example:

Week Seven

Week 7 BIG DEAL- Called to AVOID using

Client texted OMD nurse and counselor at 7:11 an1 PST to say, "I'm tired and wanna get high right now." OMD nurse responds to this by say-ing, *"Are you going to work today? Hang in there and make it to work first. Then let's set another goal after that. You're likely tired from the weekend, and that was the fun part that you can remember and work through being tired. Do you want to talk to the counselor about your feelings, too?"*

Client says he is at work already and he has already texted the counselor..'

He states he is using his support network and talks with his coworker as well. OMD nurse tells him that this is good, and that we are here for him, and she is *proud* of him for reaching out She told him to feel free to check in more today if he finds this helpful. He said he would.

At 11:37 PST, the OMD nurse messaged him to ask how he was doing and he responded that he was *"Doing okay, and that now I am busy work-ing, I'm glad I told you and my counselor."* The OMD nurse told him she was glad too and then encouraged him to make it through work, and then he can go home and get some rest. He then told the nurse more about his weekend.

NOTE:

The OMD nurse is not a psychiatric nurse, but has excellent bedside manner, and genuine curiosity. A Peer counselor can also play this role in a client's life, and I always assign a peer in residential treatment. I did not have this resource in my own program as I operate out of my private practice. If you have the means to do this, I strongly encourage it!

C. Assessment

After the first full week, I shift our weekly individual session to include spending time beginning the ASAM Assessment. For the ASAM form I

use in Santa Clara County:
https://www.sccgo v. o r g /sites/bhd-p/EHR/unicare/Pages/SUTS-Forms. aspx.

I usually do the ASAM over two sessions because I largely see it as a conversation and engagement tool. In addition to information gathering, I am learning their patterns, narrative structure, levels of insight, readiness to change, defensive structure, attachment approach... my head is busy in there!

Part of the process to is explain and show to them the ASAM and explain each of the six areas to them, and what I am thinking about as I am creating a holistic picture of them. I will write up my assessment and we will review it together. This is always interesting, especially as most of them have never seen an addiction assessment even if they have several prior episodes. They have answered the questions, but never knew the results!

I draw up my observations in a draft treatment plan model, as seen below, to give them and begin to discuss their final plan.

SAMPLE PLANS

Client R.B.

Stated or Identified Motivation for Treatment (What is the most important thing the clients wants you to help them with?)

He is seeking treatment because partner and boys are upset when he disappears. Usually, 1-2 months at a time when using. Has been relapsing since discharging probation in March. Last use meth use was 5/13/22, though drinks 1 beer 4x a week and cannabis nightly to sleep.

I. Current Placement Dimension Rating (See Dimensions below 1 - 6) Stage of Change: PreC, Cont, Prep, Action

Dim 1 Action (1) Withdrawal consists of sleeping and irritability.

Dim 2 Action (1) Needs a primary MD, MAT/Psych evaluation recommended.

Dim 3 Prep   (2) Craving may be expressed as anxiety; reports self as "high strung."

Dim 4 Cont   (3) Is ambivalent about full abstinence.

Dim 5 Prep   (5) Has multiple treatment episodes, and unable to stop relapse cycle at this time.

Dim 6 Action   (3) Home and work is stable, though relationship is unstable due to anxious attachment coping skills and current substance use. Additional: Girlfriend is drinking heavily - states it is in response to his disappearing - and is unwilling to address this as it is not illegal.

II. What problem(s) with High and Medium severity rating are of greatest concern at this time?

ASAM3:

Problem: Ongoing sense that he is "hijacked" by stress and cannot manage his impulse to use.

Goal: Patient will recognize desire to return to use triggers and relapse sequence to better interrupt cycle when it occurs.

Action:

- Referral to MD for craving and anxiety management to support emotional regulation and impulse and R/O BiPolarII.
- Activate OverSightMD™ (OMD) Connected Therapy for daily self-awareness reporting and relapse
- management.
- Educate client on OMD Wearable RPM Sticker and Activated Sticker for immediate monitoring to develop greater awareness of physical cues preceding a return to use.
- Attend weekly Mindfulness/Nutrition support group to better manage emotional reactivity

ASAM4:

Problem: Continues to fantasize that "functional meth use" might be possible for him, and that he can find a strategy to use without consequences.

Goal: Patient will identify the advantages and disadvantages of his relapsing pattern and its impact on his stated life and family goals.

Action:

- Explore past and current impact of substance use as the relapse patterns continue, including remaining connected to treatment team via text and sessions during relapses to clarify impact of substance use on his life in "real time."

- Complete OMD Readiness to Change scale daily.

- Develop willingness to utilize care coordinator and counselor support and interrupt a return to use as he moves toward abstinence from methamphetamine.

ASAM5:

Problem: Patient continues to experience frequent return to use despite having tools to abstain.

Goal: Patient will employ harm reduction strategies as he decreases his alcohol use moving towards abstinence.

Action:

- Complete Change Plan Worksheet
- Identify relapse sequence and preceding triggers as return to use happens to clarify holes in prevention plan.
- Identify alternative distraction and mindfulness strategies to support alternatives to using.
- Develop willingness to utilize care coordinator and counselor support and interrupt a return to use as he moves toward abstinence from alcohol.

ASAM6:

Problem: Patient demonstrates disruptive emotional escalation behaviors such a commanding, yelling, using drugs and disappearing to demand attention when perceiving his girlfriend or mother as emotionally unavailable, which alienates opportunity for support and leads to isolation.

Goal: Identify reactive anxious attachment strategies used when he perceives the other person has become emotionally unavailable and decrease escalation behaviors.

Action:

- Patient will complete his daily OMD log daily to track feelings of anxiety and desire to escalate, and work with his counselor to identify perceived behaviors in others that are triggering i.e. Girl-friend drinking.

- Complete ACES, Attachment Inventory, AIAT® RFQ, Resilience inventory, Social Networking Map

- When triggered, utilize Emotional IQ skills, cognitive reflective and emotional and empathy skills, and resilience strategies for more effective relationship connection to support ongoing recovery.

Client: G.K.

Stated or Identified Motivation for Treatment (What is the most important thing the clients wants you to help them with?)

He is seeking treatment because he has been arrested for the 4th DUI with significant relapse history.

I. Current Placement Dimension Rating (See Dimensions below 1 - 6) Stage of Change: PreC, Cont, Prep, Action

Dim 1 Action (0) No current withdrawal.

Dim 2 Action (1) Arthritis of thumb and bottom of foot.

Dim 3 Prep   (2) No current craving and distress stated while in legal system. History of relapse possibly connected to unidentified and stated needs and wants.

Dim 4 Cont   (3) Is committed to abstinence in legal situation. Ambivalent afterwards.

Dim 5 Cont   (3) Has previous treatment episodes and Twelve Step experience, and able to stop while in legal structure - unsuccessful otherwise.

Dim 6 Action (3) Home and work is stable and lives with family. Primary stressor is impending legal consequences and marital/family dynamic connected to ongoing relapse cycle.

What problem(s) with High and Medium severity rating are of greatest concern at this time?

ASAM3:

Problem: History of relapse when unsupervised possibly connected to unaddressed lifestyle needs and marital dynamic.

Goal: Patient will identify impact of unaddressed emotional needs for satisfying lifestyle and supportive/connected relationship.

Action:

- Utilize the Change Plan worksheet to begin focus on shifts in lifestyle that support ongoing recovery.
- Identify boundaries and assertiveness needed to restore power balance in primary relationship.
- Wear fit bit to develop greater awareness of physical cues preceding a return to use.
- Take vitamins daily to support increase in energy and mental stamina.

ASAM4:

Problem: Ambivalent about sobriety when not under legal supervision.

Goal: Patient will identify the advantages and disadvantages of use patterns and its impact on achieving the quality of life he seeks.

Action:

- Explore past and current impact of substance use as the relapse patterns if they continue, including remaining connected to treatment team via text and sessions during relapses triggers to clarify impact of substance use on his life in "real time."
- Complete Readiness to Change scale daily in journal.
- Develop willingness to utilize counselor support and interrupt a return to use as he sustains abstinence from alcohol.

ASAM6:

Problem: Primary stressor is impending legal consequences and marital/family dynamic connected to ongoing relapse cycle.

Goal: Patient will identify life activities and goals that support an ongoing commitment to sobriety.

Action:

- Patient will complete his trigger log in response to fit bit used to track feelings of anxiety and restlessness when understimulated, faced with "empty" time and need for assertive boundaries.
- Complete ACES, Attachment Inventory, AIAT RFQ, Resilience inventory.
- When triggered, utilize Emotional IQ skills, cognitive and emotional empathy skills, and resilience strategies for more effective relationship connections to support ongoing recovery.
- Attend weekly support group with counselor for co-regulation and attachment style recognition practice

Client M.L.

Stated or Identified Motivation for Treatment (What is the most important thing the clients wants you to help them with?)

He is seeking treatment because he has been unable to achieve long term sobriety.

Current Placement Dimension Rating (See Dimensions below 1 - 6) Stage of Change: PreC, Cont, Prep, Action

Dim 1 Action (2) Withdrawal irritability, grumpy, medically stable.

Dim 2 Action (0) Health is good.

Dim 3 Prep   (3) Craving may be expressed as anxiety, irritability. Long term history of depression and anxiety with occasional outbursts. Suicidal ideation

Dim 4 Cont   (3) Is ambivalent about full abstinence.

Dim 5 Cont   (3) Has previous treatment episode and Twelve Step experience, and unable to stop relapse cycle at this time.

Dim 6 Action   (3) Home and work is stable, though lives alone. Work is an ongoing stressor.

Primary stressor is lack of meaning and purpose, and need for engaged lifestyle and structure. Needs a life worth the effort of sobriety. Needs to engage internal signals for direction rather than external structure.

What problem(s) with High and Medium severity rating are of greatest concern at this time?

ASAM3:

Problem: Ongoing sense that he is "hijacked" by depression anxiety symptoms stripping motivation to move forward in self-care activities and work.

Goal: Patient will stabilize depression and anxiety to provide the energy required to act on his own behalf in self-care and satisfying life activities.

Action:

- Referral to MD for craving and depression/anxiety management to support emotional regulation and reduce suicide ideation.
- Wear RPM biosticker with daily log to develop greater awareness of physical cues preceding a return to use.
- Take vitamins daily to support increase in energy and mental stamina.
- Create daily structure

ASAM4:

Problem: Ambivalent about effort needed to obtain sobriety when struggling with depression and anxiety symptoms.

Goal: Patient will identify the advantages and disadvantages of unabated depression and use pattern and its impact on achieving the quality of life he seeks.

Action:

- Explore past and current impact of substance use as the relapse patterns continue, including remaining connected to treatment team via text and sessions during relapses to clarify impact of substance use on his life in "real time."
- Complete AIAT® Adapted Life Areas Rating,
- Develop willingness to utilize care coordinator and counselor support and interrupt a return to use as he moves toward abstinence from alcohol.

ASAM5:

Problem: Patient continues to experience frequent return to use despite having tools to abstain.

Goal: Patient will employ harm reduction strategies as he decreases his alcohol use moving towards abstinence.

Action:

- Complete Change Plan Worksheet
- Identify alternative distraction and mindfulness strategies to support alternatives to using.
- Explore triggers for cooccurring disorders from attachment style perspective
- Complete daily readiness to change ruler in journal for mental health and substance use disorders

ASAM6:

Problem: Primary stressor is lack of meaning and purpose, and need for engaged lifestyle and structure. Needs a life worth the effort of sobriety.

Goal: Patient will identify life activities and goals, which includes internal direction, that support an ongoing commitment to sobriety.

Action:

- Patient will complete his daily OMD log daily to track feelings of anxiety and restlessness when faced with "empty" time and emotional overwhelm.
- Complete ACES, Attachment Inventory, AIAI RFQ, Resilience inventory.
- When triggered, utilize Emotional IQ skills, cognitive and emotional empathy skills, and resilience strategies for more effective relationship connection to support ongoing recovery.
- Referral to trainer to develop disciplined and directed anger management workout.
- Kickboxing and boxing training.
- Attend weekly support group with counselor for co-regulation and attachment style recognition practice.

As you will notice, the goal is to have the plan be as personal to them as possible and let them edit as they will. The ASAM is a fairly effective tool, so most of the time I was accurate in my preliminary draft and had small edits. Also keep in mind that you can add to the plan as you go and more get revealed. As we say in treatment, the "real client" shows up in about 3 weeks!

D. ONGOING ASSESSMENT

Once the ASAM is completed there are other screenings embedded in the psychoeducation material. For example, early on we administer the ACE's Questionnaire for the client, and we can then review their score and our concern about the physical impact of such long-term stress on their immune system.

If they are more visual and auditory learners, you could recommend: How Childhood Trauma Affects Health Across a Lifetime I Nadine Burke Harris I TED (Youtube.com) *or* Dr. Vincent Felitti: Reflections on the Adverse Childhood Experiences (ACE) Study_(Youtube.com)

Throughout the program, I have embedded short assessments, such as the AIAT® Adapted Life Areas Rating, which *is* a way to discuss the possible presence of co-occurring disorders and help the client connect the dots between mental health and substance use across various areas of their lives.). I also have them complete the Responses to Stressful Experiences Scale.

EMOTIONAL REGULATION

The next point in treatment will be to address current and needed Emotional Regulation skills, and, if we want greater physical and emotional well-being and increase our emotional resilience, we can use sounds, feelings, sights, tastes, and smells to balance and heal ourselves. You may want to consider asking them to create a Sensory Toolbox to keep handy during the course of therapy to assist them as they move through the process. It will be necessary for them to agree to try some type of mindfulness or regulation processes. It could be listening for a few minutes at night to the How We Feel app, CALM app, or the Safe and Sound Protocol that I received training to provide. It involves listening to vibrationally altered music to better regulate their polyvagal system. In fact, I brought it into the individual therapy session to learn to co-regulate with me, and then integrated 15 minutes of the protocol into each group so they could practice co-regulating with each other while they colored. The goal is to lower their hyperarousal system, so they have more access to their frontal lobe logic and planning. They need skills to interrupt the frequent emotional hijacking that leads to fight, flight, or freeze responses. They cannot apply what they are learning if they are stuck in the limbic system.

Even if you do not formally use the Sound and Safe Protocol (SSP), introducing them to the polyvagal system, and teaming to identify their emotional regulation triggers will be incredibly important moving forward. Avoidant clients, in particular, benefit from a cognitive understanding of the changes they are making to help them tolerate the discomfort of trying the new behavior. The Polyvagal Flip Chart by Deb Dana is a wonderful tool.

ATTACHMENT ASSESSMENT

At some point in the process, you will be ready to assess their attachment style, and you can use the Experience in Close Relationship (ECR) questionnaire (APPENDIX) and review the results. It would be helpful to do a relationship history from the attachment style perspective, and they will increasingly begin to see it as it plays out in work relationships, friendships, and intimate relationships. It would be helpful to review the Attachment Style Strategies handout (APPENDIX) with the client as they discuss their current relationship challenges and help them begin to pinpoint ways that THEY act out their style. My favorite video to show and discuss with them is: How Childhood Trauma Leads to Addiction - Gabor Mate (youtube.com).

A QUICK REVIEW:

*Beyond establishing the counseling relationship as a secure base, Dallas and Vetere[126] suggest a focus on exploring - identifying attachment dilemmas and ambivalence in their current relationships such as **attachment threats, attachment fears, attachment injuries, attachment longings, and divided loyalties.** These are all key triggers to a return to substance use. Empathic failures, inevitable in the treatment context, provide the opportunity to be worked through and repaired.*

For example:

Case Note:

Client triggered to use - recognizing that feelings of betrayal from coworkers and girlfriend's emotional absence creates **so** much anxiety for him he thinks of using. Tearful about relational stress, and relieved that we will be meeting as a couple. States, *"It's easier for me to be angry. I hate admitting I'm "needy."* Reframed him as not needy, but values connection and it is a priority to him. Practiced ways to address his genuine concerns versus nitpicking and arguing over side issues.

REFLEXIVE FUNCTIONING:

A QUICK REVIEW:

After identifying the attachment areas of concern, it is impor-tant to explore alternate perceptions and behaviors that will promote change and supporting relational and emotional risk taking in real time. Acknowledging the risks of change and the threats to the percep-tions of self and others loosens the attachment dilemmas. The goal is to develop the resilience to stay connected to others when there are ruptures and conflicts to maintain the long-term relations necessary for ongoing sobriety.

It is time to assess the client's capacity for the reflexive self-func-tion (RSF), which reflects a person's capacity for inner speech and insight. We can begin to explore the resident's capacity for *Explicit Reflexive Functioning, which is a state in which individuals are able to explicitly think and speak about mental states.* One way to do this is to use a structured assessment, like the RFQ to assess for the client's ability mentalize, or identify the eternal world of others and reflect it back accurately.

The Reflexive Functioning Questionnaire is complicated to score and most often used for research purposes. I adapted it to my own use for AIAT® purposes SEE APPENDIX), and so I want to be clear that my version is not by any means a statistically evaluated instrument. I pro-vide this assessment as a means to foster conversation with the client about ways their emotional functioning hijacks and interrupt their con-nections with significant people in their lives.

A QUICK REVIEW:

The goal of taking the RFQ is to identify evidence of resident hypo-mentalizing (intolerance of others perspectives and avoiding others perspectives) to hyper-mentalizing, which is evidenced by hyperattention to their own internal reality, without strong connection to external reality. Both ends of the continuum interrupt a resident's capacity for perspective taking, empathy, identification with fictitious characters, and awareness of their own personal distress. These qualities are essential for strong attachment formation, and means we can foster the development of those specific abilities while simultaneously supporting the development of general reflective capacities.

The point of assessing current RFQ is to begin to introduce more effective metacognitive skills clients need to develop and maintain relationships. As clients begin practicing new metacognitive strategies for more effective communication and connections, they begin to demonstrate four markers of increased self-reflection skills:

1. Accurate recognition of their emotions.
2. Accurate recognition of the emotions in others.
3. Ability to accurately feel what it would be like to be in that person's position.
4. Based on the above, ability to adjust their own behavior accordingly to achieve strengthened attachments with members of their recovery support system.

Let's see how this works with client care:

Took 2-3 hits of meth last night when moving my incarcerated friend's car, and found a pipe. Threw it away.

Sequence:

- 2 days prior: Frustrated that girlfriend was drinking, and jealous that he wasn't using.
- Night before using:
- RPM biosticker lost charge. No data to [*OMD nurse*] "No one is watching"
- Ran out of Clonidine and Gabapentin - would pick it up the next day.

- Woke up stressed about money for expensive car repair and moving. Was going to work for a few weeks to get extra money, and boss called to tell him he did not have work for him. Then the So.Cal. boss called and asked him to run a job up in the Bay area over a weekend and would give him $3,000. He would need to get a crew together - so he started calling around.

- Shoulders tense, wound up **and he still went to his support group**.

- Though car had previously been cleaned out, he went to the car to move it and saw a pipe in the passenger door. "No one would know." Took 2-3 hits and threw it away. Felt like crap.

- Went inside and confessed to girlfriend because he knew that he was acting "weird." Did not leave, and slept poorly because *"she worries when I disappear."* Has asked girlfriend to make house a Sober Living Environment for him and she has refused. *"Alcohol is not illegal,"* she says which frustrates him.

He picked up his prescription the next day.

Having nightmares about going to jail again, about fights in prison, and startled awake. Thinks his unconscious is trying to keep the criminal lifestyle alive for him like an AI running in the background. Counselor and OMD nurse will keep close watch over him this weekend. He realizes this is the first time he has ever been able to see exactly how a relapse happens instead of "it just happens."

RFQ Hypermentalizing - Don't consider other's perspective

Bridging through relating, "This whole thing AIAT® is about connecting!" Considered his impact on his girlfriend. Trying to work on his hypermentalizing style.

Tearful - *"It's scary to leave it behind, Every time I doubt myself or feel betrayed by someone I care about I numb it with meth."* (primary attachment). Recognizes he cannot use "recreationally."

Assessments in the Attachment Infused Addiction Treatment® Model

- ASAM
- AIAT® MIRC
- ACE's

- Experience in Close Relationship (ECR) questionnaire
- AIAT® Life Areas Assessment
- AIAT® Reflexive Functioning
- Readiness to Change Questionnaire (Treatment Version)
- Resilience Assessment
- Social Networking Map

E. Psychoeducation

Each week we cover a different module and, depending on the discussion, it may carry into the individual therapy session the same week. The goal is to help them APPLY what we are learning and move from the cognitive rigidity or over-reactivity they have operated from into having more agency to respond to situations, a more empowering position to take.

For example, addressing internalized stigma.

When thinking about the ASAM definition of addiction states, *"It means it's treatable - but not for me,"* has been client's thinking.

For example: *"I've been told I am not trying hard enough, don't want it bad enough, and I sort of give up. When I think I sort of have a handle on it, it pops back up and kicks my ass again. I always love to use until I am miserable and forget the euphoric recall."* Relapse planning makes sense now." *I didn't try it when I was younger. Too much effort. I didn't know I would still be here 20 years later with bigger responsibilities and bigger problems. Responsibilities bother me the most when high - it snowballs. It's what everyone wants from me."*

It is normal to have internalized cultural beliefs about addiction and experience a hefty amount of denial and self-loathing about both losing control of the substance and the behaviors that have accompanied it. This is also true to mental health conditions, and at least 50% of our people have multiple issues. The counselor will need to check in on this throughout the Stages of Change, because it is incredibly hard to come to peace with this, and it takes time. It certainly will not be settled for the client in the first year of sobriety.

Cognitive Challenges in Early Recovery

I wanted to take a moment and note the cognitive reality of early recovery and its impact on psychoeducation. In general, research has indicated that about 65% of folks coming from the criminal justice system have a history of learning disability or ADHD/ADD, and maybe a TBI.

FUNCTIONALLY: They may present themselves as having learning challenges even if only temporarily, and so when presenting the psychoeducation material, it is important to think of MULTI-MODAL learning. It is quite possible that your client may not learn as well with traditional reading and writing approaches, and assessing their learning style will create stronger treatment plans. While I provide the written material to them, I have learned it well enough to discuss the concepts without having to read it to them or have them read. They are able to take it home for review.

I am primarily working through the material for **application** purposes. This is possible because I am delivering the material to them individually and not in a group format, so I can tailor it to them, and throw in videos as well to make a point if they are more visual learners. Some of them will want to read it in entirety and others will not. Interestingly, they did not lose the binder between sessions and brought it with them every week. I found this particularly amusing because residents lose their binders in a residential treatment program all the time and they aren't even leaving the building!

When thinking of cognitive problems, it is useful to remember that no human skills operate in isolation. We depend on a combination of several skills to carry out individual tasks. For example, if we want to remember what someone is saying to us, we first have to be able to:

- Attend to what they are saying (concentration)
- Understand what they are saying (language/information-processing)
- Keep up with the flow of conversation (speed of thought)

It might be useful for you to keep these timelines in mind:

A Timeline for Cognitive Recovery after Abstinence at 2 Weeks of Abstinence

The average recovering alcoholic experiences:

- Increased confusion
- Increased irritability
- Distractibility
- A decreased ability to attend and concentrate
- Slower reaction times
- A decreased ability to use verbal abstract reasoning
- Decreased verbal short-term memory
- Impaired verbal learning abilities
- Impaired mental flexibility
- Impaired visual-spatial abilities
- Decreased non-verbal short-term memory

By 2 Months

By 60 days into recovery, distractibility, confusion and irritability have disappeared, but memory problems, concentration, learning, mental flexibility, abstract reasoning and visual-spatial deficits remain. (Still only 8+ weeks.)

From 2 months - 5 years of abstinence people make incredible cognitive gains and get very close to a full restoration of normal functioning.

By 5 years, the average alcoholic may still experience:

- Problems with non-verbal abstract reasoning and non-verbal short-term memory
- Diminished mental flexibility
- Diminished visual-spatial abilities

I am not going to include the full binder here because it is copywritten, though I will include a sample module so you can see the overall presentation.

SAMPLE PSYCHOEDUCATION MODULE

Will It Be Worth It To Change?

Last week I asked you what you would GET if you reduced or stopped using substances, and I thought today would be a good time to ask you whether or not you think it would be worth it? You have tried to quit before, it didn't work, and it's possible you are not so sure this time will be different, even if you are part of this new approach. I don't blame you.

Maybe it would be helpful if we talked about how change normally works, what famous psychotherapist Virginia Satir called "The Process of Change" so you can see the larger picture.

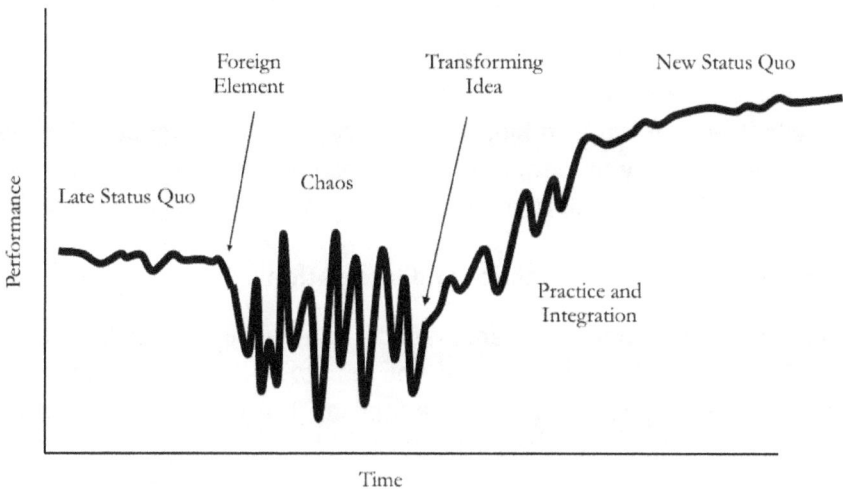

Late Status Quo

Before we start changing anything, drug use or gambling, we have been doing what we are doing for a very long time. Satir says it is like we are stuck in concrete, and the way we are living has become so normal it is just "the way it is."

Can you relate to feeling you are an addict, have always been one, and probably always will be?

It would stay that way unless stage two happens:

Introduction of a Foreign Element

Something happens to break up the norm. You get arrested, CPS, you are threatened with divorce, your family does an intervention, your doctor says you have developed a heart condition...

What interrupted YOUR drug use?

A lot of us didn't want it, didn't see it coming, aren't so happy to be here. YOUR common Foreign Element is ....

CHAOS

When you are first disrupted, everything feels out of control, you aren't sure what will happen next, a lot of anxiety can happen... like the floor underneath you is moving.

Can you relate to this feeling? How about NOW?

This is a key time, because if we don't move to the next level, we get so uncomfortable that we run back to the status quo - the concrete we were in. Even if it is miserable, it is a misery we know. Virginia Satir says that doing this is why people fail in counseling. The key is to hang in there and allow yourself to move forward to the next stages.

Transforming Idea and Practice and Integration

This is the time when you start practicing and using new skills and try new behaviors. It is uncomfortable, you tend to be dorky at it, and again, the temptation is to go back to the familiar. The Attachment program was set up to allow more than the 30-day window to buy you the time to work through this stage and next one instead of ending your treatment too soon in the change cycle.

Can you think of a time that you hung in there when you felt vulnerable and wound up on the other side more confident?

By the time you have finished these two stages you will go to the final stage.

New Status Quo

Using the new skills you are learning will feel more natural, and you find yourself handling situations well that used to create serious panty wadding.

Satir says we need at least three of these cycles to feel we are actually different people, we have really changed. The longer time with us is going to allow you to do this, if you want to.

Again, keep thinking about what you GET and who you want to be when you move to the next level of treatment.

What Stage of Change Are You In?

I thought it might be useful to see where you are in the process right now. Sort of setting your baseline and seeing where you go from here. The theorists. Prochaska and DiClemente said that we move through predictable stages of change along the way to deciding to take action and keep the change we make. You are going to move back and forth through them while you are here and after, so maybe it will help to recognize yourself when you do.

Precontemplation:

Simply put, "Life is the Problem," and "Drug use is the Solution." If my life didn't suck, I wouldn't need to use. Besides, I can control it and stop any time I want to. I certainly don't need someone else to tell me to change.

In Virginia Satir's model, you are in what stage? Late Status Quo.

Honestly, have you have started treatment programs before thinking like this? How about coming into AIAT® this time? Keep it real, if you're willing.

These stages aren't just about addiction, but apply to ANY change like losing weight, getting a relationship, changing jobs...

Contemplation

Okay, there might be a problem, sometimes it gets out of hand. I only get locked up when I use, so maybe I should cut down or stop using. I am not sure it is bad enough to accept help, though. Maybe I can just stop on my own.

In Virginia Satir's model, some problem has happened to shake things up, so makes us start to wonder if Drug Use might be the problem and not Life.

What about you? What would need to happen, or HAS happened to make you wonder if drug use might be the problem?

Preparation

Ok, I have a problem and I should probably do something about it. I tried to stop myself but something always happens...Virginia Satir's Chaos, perhaps? So, I need a PLAN that will work this time. I need help.

Maybe you, by any chance? My experience is that we shift between Contemplation and Preparation, unsure if we actually need HELP to change. It's a hard one. Have you noticed this?

Action

The mistake treatment has always made is to treat every single resident as though they are in the stage of change, and then set them up to either lie to us in order to get out, or to fail as soon as they leave.

This is Virginia Satir's *Transforming Idea and Practice and Integration.* We are actively doing new behavior, and sustaining it for six months moving through the process of change.

I am hoping that as you stay with me for this longer period of time, you will pay attention to where you might be with each new change you are making. For example, you might be in precontemplation or contemplation about your mental health issues, but action about your meth use. There is another stage you enter after you have been in Action for six months.

Maintenance

In this stage, you are continuing to use the new skills you have been developing and are adding new ones in the outpatient and aftercare process to strengthen and deepen the changes you have made. It is our hope that once you leave Pathways residential and IOP you will be here, and it will include the support of other people.

The goal while you are with us is to be as honest as you can with your individual counselor, and even the group, about where you are in the process and let us help if we can.

TOPICS COVERED in PSYCHOEDUCATION MODULES

- Why does the ability to develop solid relationships in recovery matter?

- Will it be worth it to change?

- Process of change and Stages Change

- Emotional Regulation - SSP

- Change Plan

- Overview of Attachment Styles

- Overview of ASAM and DSM5 definition of addiction Developmental basis of attachment

- Attachment style strategies Attachment and emotional regulation Attachment and immune system Addiction and the immune system Resilience in recovery

- Emotional intelligence Components of empathy

- Inhabiting your body

- Social network mapping

- Behavioral addictions, including relationships Post-Acute Withdrawal

- Relationship Rupture and Repair

- Relationship based Relapse Prevention Planning

F. IDENTIFYING AND INCREASING SOCIAL SUPPORT

Developing A Social Network Map

Our next point in treatment is to begin to identify the people in our client's current world and the various ways they might be available to participate in their lives. This means constructing the Social Network Map I have included in the book, and completing the chart, and then the Recovery Village. It is at this point that we need to start encouraging the client to begin to attend an outside support group if they are willing. While Twelve Step groups are plentiful and free, there are other choices like SMART Recovery, LifeRing, Women for Sobriety, and Celebrate Recovery through their church. They may decide to join a formal group therapy conducted by a therapist. It may be that they decide to join a volunteer organization and participate in that type of group format. The bottom line is that we need them to have a laboratory to take their new skills on the road!

It is at this point that our own transparency and feedback **will** be vital, as we will need to serve as reality testing and offer a safe place to role play. (SEE SOCIAL NETWORKING DATA RECORDING SHEET IN APPENDIX.)

Recovery Village

Using colored pens, -write the names or initials around the "hut." Draw a line between the people in the network who talk to each other about you.

Next to each appropriate hut have the resident list the initials and phone number for the support person.

G. IDENTIFYING RELAPSE TRIGGERS

Relapse Prevention Planning

There will come a point when the client is more effectively using their social world more effectively to manage their internal distress when triggered, as well as their own emotional regulations skills. It will be key that they become adept at identifying and ANTICIPATING triggers as they move through the world. Hopefully they will have sharpened their ability to tune into their physical cues for hints that they may need to take care of themselves or address their discomfort in a productive way. This is particularly true for attachment triggers, and we will spend a good portion of time developing with the client a clear list of triggers and effective responses. You will do this in writing for them to both have for later reference and share with their support system. I have provided one model, but there are many others you may choose to adopt.

A NOTE ABOUT RELATIONSHIP REPAIR

Now that you and the client have identified a cast of characters to be part of their recovery plan, you need to tum your attention to ways that breaks, or ruptures, in our relationships can trigger a return to using substances. Relationship rupture and repair is the key to long term recovery from an attachment perspective. Using rupture as a chance to deepen a connection and be seen and heard is vital.

This is another psychoeducation opportunity, because relationship rupture needs to be normalized, as does repair. The AIAT® clientele rarely have models for this, which is why their attachment strategies are so pervasive across their relationships. Fortunately, this is not an intuitive skill, but one which can be taught once they can identify ways in which their defensive strategies might be impacting others in their lives.

Basic rupture repair skills include:

Respect

Show respect to your partner by reaching out to him or her, whether you think you were right or wrong in the situation. They may or may not be able to respond immediately depending on their own reactivity and distress.

Showing respect for my partner's thoughts is essential to a great relationship, especially whenever you disagree. And taking turns when you finally do begin to talk is what heals people and their relationships because they feel seen and heard.

It is important to understand that you can only change *your* own behavior. It is not your role to correct or criticize your partner's behavior.

Ownership

Take responsibility for how you contributed to the pain in the relationship, no matter where it is between 1% and 100%. For example, you might start off the conversation by saying:

"I'd like to take responsibility for my actions last night. I could have informed you that I was coming home late and couldn't make it to dinner at your family's house. I imagine you felt worried, angry, and embarrassed that I wasn't there." (Recognizing that you impact people who care about you is critical for mentalizing and connecting)

The first step is acknowledging your part in the problem, even if you can't identify any specific role yet.

Curiosity

Maintain an attitude of curiosity when talking, especially when receiving their thoughts and emotions. Try to be genuinely interested in hearing your partner's side of the story. And *remain* curious even if that story doesn't align with your own.

"I'd like to know what happened that night. Can you tell me what you need from me to heal and what I should have done differently that night?"

Don't assume you know what your partner wants.

Your goal is simply to receive information when your job is to listen. And your goal is to give information when it's your turn to share. Depending on the severity of the rupture, it may take more than one conversation.

Vulnerability

Allowing yourself to be vulnerable is hard when you're feeling hurt or defensive.

Decide to relax your defenses. Let go of your (false) need to "be right". This choice allows you the freedom and strength to fully understand your partner's world and to empathize with their pain. When both partners are vulnerable with one another, you will strengthen your connection.

Compassion

Listen with your whole body, which means your head and your heart. Every story has two sides. And no one is perfect.

Be kind, even if you are feeling hurt or blamed. Try to put yourself in your partner's shoes with open-mindedness as you listen, so you can imagine the situation from their perspective.

Imagine how they might have felt emotionally both when it happened and afterwards. If you find yourself ready to criticize or be defensive, take a moment to refocus your intention on being compassionate.

Making Amends Means Changing Behavior

Demonstrate a willingness to change your behavior based on your partner's feedback. If you continue engaging in behavior that is hurtful to your partner, the problem won't go away.

Try to express Behavior Changes Requests that are positive, measurable, and specific. Accept Behavior Changes Requests as a great opportunity for mutual healing and growth.

It is always important to understand that what your partner needs may *not* be what you would need in this situation. And that's okay. You are separate AND connected.

H. FINAL ASSESSMENTS

When the client is concluding their first 90 days, it is an excellent time to do some quick assessments to have a guide for the focus in individual counseling and group for the next 90 days of the program.

HAVE THEM PULL OUT THEIR RECOVERY VILLAGES.

I want you to provide some scenarios that are of concern to you that we can practice using your recovery village to respond to.

How Likely Are you to USE your Recovery Village?

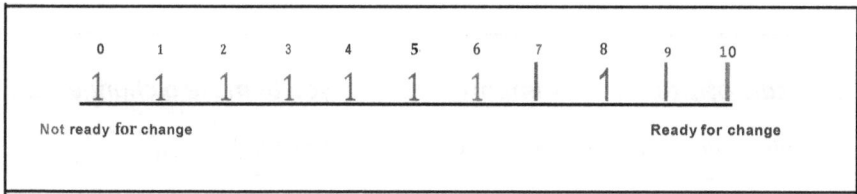

0	1	2	3	4	5	6	7	8	9	10

Not ready for change   Ready for change

Let's Check Your Ability to Read Yourself: Re-TAKE the RFQ

Lets' Check in On Relationship Management

How are you doing with Basic Skills to develop trusted relationships include:

1. Awareness of the state of mind of self and others.

2. Monitoring the accuracy of our state of mind (which means checking in with ourselves and the other person to make sure we don't have slewed thinking).

3. Awareness of one's own influence on the other's state or behavior, and vice versa (How am I affecting others?).

4. Becoming aware of one's state of mind in such a way that it has an emotional regulation effect on us (paying attention to my physical and emotional state to manage myself).

5. Awareness of one's own or another's action plans and goal directedness. (This means checking in with myself and the other person and SHARING.)

6. Finding meaning in our experiences. *(We feel that WE and our participation matter.)*

Where is Your Stage of Change for:

Substances?

Mental Health treatment?

Physical Maintenance and Inhabiting your Body?

Readiness Ruler

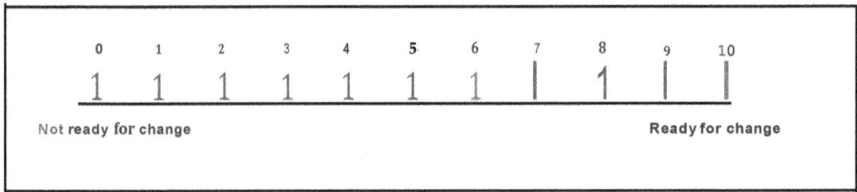

On a scale of 1 to 10, how important is it to you to make a change in...?

Example, If you are a 5, why are you a 5 and not a 3?

Or if you are a 5, what need to happen for you to go to a 7? How could I assist you in getting to a 7?

Finally, we review the Feedback Form for Client Experience

Overall Assessment of the AIAT® Model:

1. What stage of change are you as you leave treatment?

    PreC, Cont, Prep, Action

2. What stage did you START treatment in?

    PreC, Cont, Prep, Action

3. Why do you think you moved to another stage or DID NOT move to another stage? _____
_____
_____
_____
_____
_____

4. What Attachment Style are you? _____

5. How do you know that this is your style? _____
   _____
   _____
   _____
   _____

6. How hard was it to create your Recovery Village? _____

7. What would get in the way of USING your village? _____
   _____
   _____
   _____
   _____
   _____
   _____

8. What was the most helpful part of the AIAT® Model for you? __
   _____
   _____
   _____
   _____
   _____
   _____

9. What was the LEAST helpful part of the AIAT® Model for you? __
   _____
   _____
   _____
   _____
   _____
   _____

10. Would be willing to have us follow-up with you and check in to
    see how you are doing in 3 months, 6 months, and one year from
    now? If so, what number and email should we use?_____
    _____
    _____
    _____
    _____

Resident Signature _____

Date _____

Conclusion

The Attachment Infused Addiction Treatment® Model has provided a foundational roadmap in my addiction treatment process for several years, and it is heart-warming when someone says, *"I am not dreading coming to counseling like I usually do. I'm kind if excited to learn about this "connecting" thing!"* That does not mean that their process will be easy, and the recognition of the impact of interrupted attachment on so many of their adult life decisions can weigh heavily at times.

My own early childhood attachment disruption weighs on me at times when I still see its impact in that split-second reaction to distance before I see it and counter it. When I reflect on those in my life who have achieved long-term sobriety, I am struck repeatedly by the quality of the relational support in their lives, and I am heartened to know that the capacity to trust and include others when in distress can be learned. Where substances may have been our only solution at one time in our lives, the Attachment Infused Addiction Treatment® Model provides a way to develop the skills needed to have a reality-based shot at life-sustaining connections with others. I truly help this model will be helpful in your own work with those who struggle to form the connections we need in order to sustain long-term recovery.

If you decide you would like to implement the AIAT® model as I have designed and use it, you can contact me for licensing opportunities so you can have a copy of the binder. You an arrange for AIAT® training, and all of the assessments as well.

marycook@connectionscounselingassociates.com

You are also welcome to adapt the material in the book to your currently exiting program, especially if you have clinicians grounded in the attachment theory underlying the model. If you do, let me know how it's going!

RESOURCES

1. Khantzian, E., Albanese, M.,Lanham, Md., Rowman and Little-field, (2008   American Journal of Psychiatry, Volume 166, Number 11, pp. 192

2. Bowlby, J. (1988). *A secure base: Clinical applications of attachment theory*. London: Routledge.

3. Ibid.

4. Coan, J. A. (2011). The Social Regulation of Emotion. In J. Decety & J. T. Cacioppo (Eds.), *Handbook of Social Neuroscience* (pp. 614–623). New York: Oxford University Press.

5. Waters, S. F., Virmani, E. A., Thompson, R. A., Meyer, S., Raikes, H. A., & Jochem, R. (2010). Emotion regulation and attachment: Unpacking two constructs and their association. *Journal of Psychopathology and Behavioral Assessment, 32*(1), 37–47.

6. Laible, D. J., & Thompson, R. A. (2000). Mother-Child Discourse, Attachment Security, Shared Positive Affect, and Early Conscience Development. *Child Development, 71*(5), 1424–1440.

7. Raikes, H. A., & Thompson, R. A. (2008). Attachment security and parenting quality predict children's problem-solving, attributions, and loneliness with peers. *Attachment and Human Development, 10*(3), 319–344.

8. Thompson, R. A. (2016). Early Attachment and Later Development: Reframing the Question. In J. Cassidy & P. R. Shaver (Eds.), *Handbook of Attachment* (3. Edition, pp. 330–348). New York/London: Guilford Press.

9. Ainsworth, M. D. (1991). Attachment and other affectional bonds across the life cycle. In C. M. Parkes, J. Stevenson-Hinde, & P. Marris (Eds.), *Attachment across the life cycle* (pp. 33–51). New York: Routledge.

10. Allen, J. G., Fonagy, P., Bateman, A. Jon G. Allen, Peter Fonagy, Anthony Bateman. (2008). Mentalizing in Clinical Practice. American Psyciatric Pub.

11. Ibid.

12. Neger, Emily N., & Prinz, Ronald J. (2015).   Interventions to Address Parenting and Parental Substance Abuse: Conceptual

and Methodological Considerations. Clinical psychology review 39:71-82

13. Söderström, K., & Skårderud, F. (2009). Minding the baby. Mentalization-based treatment in families with parental substance use disorder: Theoretical framework. *Nordic Psychology, 61*(3), 47-65.

14. Ainsworth, M., Blehar, M. C., Waters, E., & Wall, S. (1978). Patterns of Attachment: A Psychological Study of the Strange Situation. Hillsdale, NJ: Lawrence Erlbaum Associates.

15. Becker, L., Coan, J., Hasselmo, K. (2013). Familiarity promotes the blurring of self and other in the neural representation of threat. *Social Cognitive and Affective Neuroscience*, Volume 8, Issue 6, Pages 670–677

16. Lazarus, R. S., & Folkman, S. (1984). Stress,appraisal, and coping. New York: Springer. https://www.simplypsychology.org/stress-management.html

17. Epstein, S., & Meier, P. (1989). Constructive thinking: A broad coping variable with specific components. *Journal of Personality and Social Psychology, 57*(2), 332-350.

18. Heider, F. (1958). The psychology of interpersonal relations. New York: Wiley

19. Bowlby, J. (1973). Attachment and loss, Vol. 2: Separation: Anxiety and anger. New York: Basic Books.

20. Coan, J. A., Schaefer, H. S., & Davidson, R. J. (2006). Lending a Hand. Psychological Science, 17(12), 1032–1039.

21. Mikulincer, M., & Shaver, P. R. (2007). Attachment in adulthood: Structure, dynamics, and change. New York: Guilford Publications Inc.

22. Miller, J. B., & Stiver, I. P. (1997). The healing connection: How women form relationships in therapy and in life. Boston, MA, US: Beacon Press.

23. Agishtein, P. & Brumbaugh, C. (2013). Cultural Variation in Adult Attachment: The Impact of Ethnicity, Collectivism, and Country of Origin. Journal of Social, Evolutionary, and Cultural Psychology, 7(4), 384-405.

24. van Ijzendoorn, M. H., & Sagi, A. (1999). Cross-cultural patterns

of attachment: Universal and contextual dimensions. In J. Cassidy & P. R. Shaver (Eds.), *Handbook of attachment: Theory, research, and clinical applications* (pp. 713-734). New York, NY, US: The Guilford Press.

25. Crittenden, Patricia.(2006) A Dynamic-Maturational Model of Attachment. Australian and New Zealand Journal of Family Therapy, Volume27, Issue2 Pages 105-115

26. Gillath, O., Selcuk, E., Shaver, P.R.(2008). Moving Toward a Secure Attachment Style: Can Repeated Security Priming Help? Social and Personality Psychology Compass 2(4):1651 - 1666

27. Gillath, O., Hart, J., Noftle, E. E., & Stockdale, G. D. (2009). Development and validation of a state adult attachment measure (SAAM). *Journal of Research in Personality, 43*(3), 362-373.

28. Seigel, Daniel J.(2015) The Developing Mind, Second Edition: How Relationships and the Brain Interact to Shape Who We Are Second Edition. The Guilford Press; Second edition

29. Schore, A. N. (1994). Affect regulation and the origin of the self: The neurobiology of emotional development. Hillsdale, NJ, US: Lawrence Erlbaum Associates, Inc.

30. Schore, A. N. (1996). The experience-dependent maturation of a regulatory system in the orbital prefrontal cortex and the origin of developmental psychopathology. Development and Psychopathology, 8(1), 59-87.

31. Schore, A. N.(2009).Relational trauma and the developing right brain: an interface of psychoanalytic self psychology and neuroscience. Ann N Y Academic Science. 59:189-203

32. Siegel, Daniel J. (2009) Toward an interpersonal neurobiology of the developing mind: Attachment relationships, "mindsight," and neural integration Issue Online: 09 January 2003

33. Panksepp, Jaak & Biven, Lucy. (2012) *The Archaeology of Mind.* W. W. Norton & Company; 1 edition, p. 17

34. Schore, Allen N. (2012) The Science of the Art of Psychotherapy (Norton Series on Interpersonal Neurobiology) 1st Edition. W. W. Norton & Company

35. Gill, Richard (Ed.). (2014) Addictions From An Attachment Perspective.Karnac Books, Ltd., London.p.63

36. Bowlby, J. (1982). Attachment and loss, Vol. 1: Attachment (2nd ed.). New York: Basic Books.

37. Cassidy, J., & Kobak, R. R. (1988). Avoidance and its relation to other defensive processes. In J. Belsky & T. Nezworski (Eds.), *Child psychology. Clinical implications of attachment* (pp. 300-323). Hillsdale, NJ, US: Lawrence Erlbaum Associates, Inc.

38. Shaver, P. R., & Mikulincer, M. (2002). Attachment-related psycho-dynamics. Attachment & Human Development, 4(2), 133–161.

39. Shaver, P. R., & Mikulincer, M. (2007). Adult attachment strategies and the regulation of emotion. In J. J. Gross (Ed.), Handbook of Emotion Regulation. New York: Guilford Press.

40. Cassidy, J., & Kobak, R. R. (1988). Avoidance and its relation to other defensive processes. In J. Belsky & T. Nezworski (Eds.), *Child psychology. Clinical implications of attachment* (pp. 300-323). Hillsdale, NJ, US: Lawrence Erlbaum Associates, Inc.

41. Main, M. (1981). Avoidance in the service of attachment: A working paper. In K. Immelmann, G. W. Barlow, L. Petrinovich, & M. Main (Eds.), Behavioral Development: The Bielefeld Interdisciplinary Project (pp. 651–693). New York: Cambridge University Press.

42. Cassidy, J., & Kobak, R. R. (1988). Avoidance and its relation to other defensive processes. In J. Belsky & T. Nezworski (Eds.), *Child psychology. Clinical implications of attachment* (pp. 300-323). Hillsdale, NJ, US: Lawrence Erlbaum Associates, Inc.

43. Ibid.

44. Mikulincer, M., & Florian, V. (1998). The relationship between adult attachment styles and emotional and cognitive reactions to stressful events. In J. A. Simpson & W. S. Rholes (Eds.), Attachment theory and close relationships (pp. 143–165). New York: Guilford Press.

45. Shaver, P. R., Hazan, C., & Bradshaw, D. (1988). Love as attachment: The integration of three behavioral systems. In R. J. Sternberg & M. L. Barnes (Eds.), The Psychology of Love (pp. 68–99). New Haven: Yale University Press.

46. Hesse E, Main M. (2006). Frightened, threatening, and dissociative parental behavior in low-risk samples: description, discussion, and interpretations. Developmental Psychopathology. Spring;18(2):309-43.

47. Main, M., & Hesse, E. (1990). Parents' unresolved traumatic experiences are related to infant disorganized attachment status: Is frightened and/or frightening parental behavior the linking mechanism? In M. T. Greenberg, D. Cicchetti, & E. M. Cummings (Eds.), *The John D. and Catherine T. MacArthur Foundation series on mental health and development. Attachment in the preschool years: Theory, research, and intervention* (pp. 161-182). Chicago, IL, US: University of Chicago Press.

48. Main, M., & Solomon, J. (1990). Procedures for identifying infants as disorganized/disoriented during the Ainsworth Strange Situation. In M. T. Greenberg, D. Cicchetti, & E. M. Cummings (Eds.), *The John D. and Catherine T. MacArthur Foundation series on mental health and development. Attachment in the preschool years: Theory, research, and intervention* (pp. 121-160). Chicago, IL, US: University of Chicago Press.

49. Porges S. W. (2009). The polyvagal theory: new insights into adaptive reactions of the autonomic nervous system. Cleveland Clinic journal of medicine, 76 Suppl 2(Suppl 2), S86-90.

50. Maunder RG1, Hunter JJ. (2001) Attachment and psychosomatic medicine: developmental contributions to stress and disease. Psychosomatic Medicine. Jul-Aug;63(4):556-67.

51. Flores, Philp. (2011). Addiction as an Attachment Disorder. Jason Aronson, Inc. , pg. 180

52. Horvath, Adam (2005) The therapeutic relationship: Research and theory - An introduction to the Special Issue. Psychotherapy Research. 15(1-2):3-7

53. Schindler, Andreas. (2019) Attachment and Substance Use Disorders—Theoretical Models, Empirical Evidence, and Implications for Treatmen Front. Psychiatry. Sec. Addictive Disorders. (Volume 10.

54. Nakazawa, Donna Jackson. (2016) Childhood Disrupted: How Your Biography Becomes Your Biology, and How You Can Heal. Atria Books; Reprint edition

55. **Ibid.**

56. Siegel, Daniel (Purchased 2018) Interpersonal Neurobiology in Therapy, online lecture series. https://www.mindsightinstitute.com/Interpersonal-Neurobiology-in-Therapy

57. Neurobiological research and the reward–deficiency hypothesis

58. https://www.frontiersin.org/articles/10.3389/fpsyt.2019.00727/full

59. Nutt DJ, Lingford-Hughes A, Erritzoe D, Stokes PR. The dopamine theory of addiction: 40 years of highs and lows. Nat Rev Neurosci (2015) 16(5):305–12. doi: 10.1038/nrn3939 PubMed Abstract | CrossRef Full Text | Google Scholar

60. Blum K, Thanos PK, Oscar-Berman M, Febo M, Baron D, Badgaiyan RD, et al. dopamine in the brain: hypothesizing surfeit or deficit links to reward and addiction. J Reward Defic Syndr (2015) 1(3):95–104. doi: 10.17756/jrds.2015-016

61. Alvarez-Monjaras M, Mayes LC, Potenza MN, Rutherford HJ. A developmental model of addictions: integrating neurobiological and psychodynamic theories through the lens of attachment. Attach Hum Dev (2018) 18:1–22. doi: 10.1080/14616734.2018.1498113

62. Center on the Developing Child at Harvard University (2012). The Science of Neglect: The Persistent Absence of Responsive Care Disrupts the Developing Brain: Working Paper No. 12. Retrieved from www.developingchild.harvard.edu.

63. Attachment Theory – The Alcoholics Guide to Alcoholism Retrieved 8/15/23

64. Buczynski, Ruth, PhD. & Lanius, Ruth, MD, PhD Retrieved 2011. http:// nicabmstealthseminar.s3.amazonaws.com/Trauma2012/Lanius/NICABM-Lanius2012.pdf

65. Ibid.

66. Ibid.

67. Public Policy Statement: Definition of Addiction (2013) https://www.asam.org/resources/definition-of-addiction

68. *Diagnostic and Statistical Manual of Mental Disorders* (*DSM–5*) *(2013)*) American Psychiatric Publishing; 5th edition

69. G. Montero, G., González, M.S., Mondragón Egaña, Mondragon. (2016) Is social attachment an addictive disorder? Role of the latest findings in the opioid system. European Psychiatry. Volume 33, Supplement, Page S381

70. Gabor Mate. (2010) In the Realm of Hungry Ghosts: Close Encounters with Addiction. North Atlantic Books; 1 edition

71. Schindler, Andrea (2019). Attachment and Substance Use Disorders—Theoretical Models, Empirical Evidence, and Implications for Treatment. Front: Psychiatry, https://doi.org/10.3389/fpsyt.2019.00727

72. Laprairie JL, Murphy AZ. (2009) Neonatal injury alters adult pain sensitivity by increasing opioid tone in the periaqueductal gray. Front Behavioral Neuroscience.;3:31

73. Slattery D.A., Neumann, I.D. (2008) No stress please! Mechanisms of stress hyporesponsiveness of the maternal brain. Journal of Physiology. ;586(2):377-85.

74. Buczynski, Ruth, PhD. & Lanius, Ruth, MD, PhD Retrieved 2011. http:// nicabmstealthseminar.s3.amazonaws.com/Trauma2012/Lanius/NICABM-Lanius2012.pdf

75. Gill, Richard (Ed.). (2014) Addictions From An Attachment Perspective. Karnac Books, Ltd., London.p.44

76. Buczynski, Ruth, PhD. & Lanius, Ruth, MD, PhD Retrieved 2011. http:// nicabmstealthseminar.s3.amazonaws.com/Trauma2012/Lanius/NICABM-Lanius2012.pdf

77. Laprairie JL, Murphy AZ. (2009) Neonatal injury alters adult pain sensitivity by increasing opioid tone in the periaqueductal gray. Front Behavioral Neuroscience.;3:31

78. Slattery D.A., Neumann, I.D. (2008) No stress please! Mechanisms of stress hyporesponsiveness of the maternal brain. Journal of Physiology. ;586(2):377-85.

79. Brown, Stephanie (1996) Treating the Alcoholic. Wiley and Sons.

80. Brown, Stephanie. (2004) A Place Called Self. A Radical Transformation. Hazelden Publishing; First Edition

81. Ibid.

82. Groshkova T, Best D, White W. (2012). The Assessment of Recovery Capital: Properties and psychometrics of a measure of addiction recovery strengths. Drug & Alcohol Review, 1-8.

83. Cloud, W.,& Grandfield, R. (2008) Conceptualizing Recovery Capital: Expansion of a Theoretical Concept. Substance Use & Misuse 43(12-13):1971-86

84. Rec-Cap Training Model http://www.recoveryeducationnetwork.org/uploads/9/6/6/3/96633012/rec-cap_recovery_capital.pdf

85. Symonds, Paul. (2024). 5 Key Principles of Knowles Adult Learning Theory Andragogy

86. Winnicott, D. W. (1971). Playing and Reality. London: Penguin

87. SAMHSA's Concept of Trauma and Guidance for a Trauma-Informed Approach. Substance Abuse and Mental Health Services Administration (SAMHSA) SAMHSA's Concept of Trauma and Guidance for a Trauma-Informed Approach

88. Wallin, D. J. (2007). Attachment in Psychotherapy. New York, NY, US: Guilford Press.pg. 198.

89. Gill, Richard (Ed.). (2014) Addictions From An Attachment Perspective. Karnac Books, Ltd., London.p.44

90. Fonagy, P., Steele, M., Steele, H., Higgitt, A., & Target, M. (1994). The Emanuel Miller Memorial Lecture 1992: The theory and practice of resilience. *Child Psychology & Psychiatry & Allied Disciplines, 35*(2), 231-257.

91. Bateman, A., & Fonagy, P. (2010). Mentalization based treatment for borderline personality disorder. World psychiatry : official journal of the World Psychiatric Association (WPA), 9(1), 11-5.

92. Daniel P. PhD (Author), David S. Elliott, David S. PhD. (2016) Attachment Disturbances in Adults: Treatment for Comprehensive Repair 1st Edition. W. W. Norton & Company, pg. 266

93. Flores, Philp. (2011). Addiction as an Attachment Disorder. Jason Aronson, Inc. , pg. 180

94. Ibid., pg 210

95. Ibid., pg. 178

96. F Flores, P. J. (2001). Addiction as an attachment disorder: Implications for group therapy. International Journal of Group Psychotherapy, 51(1), 63-81

97. Miller, W. R., & Rollnick, S. (2002). Motivational interviewing: Preparing people for change (2nd ed.). New York, NY, US: The Guilford Press.

98. Allen, J.G. (2006): *Mentalizing in practice*. In J.G. Allen & P. Fonagy (Eds.), Handbook of Mentalization-Based Treatment (pp. 3-26). Chichester: Wiley.

99. About the CDC-Kaiser ACE Study. (Retrieved 2018) https://www.cdc.gov/violenceprevention/childabuseandneglect/acestudy/about.html

100. Seery, Mark D. (2011) Resilience: A Silver Lining to Experiencing Adverse Life Events? Current Directions in Psychological Science Vol 20, Issue 6, pp. 390 – 394, First Published December 5, 2011

101. Ibid.

102. Fraley, R. C., Waller, N. G., & Brennan, K. A. (2000). An item-response theory analysis of self-report measures of adult attachment. Journal of Personality and Social Psychology, 78, 350-365.

103. Vetere, Arlene., Dallas, Rudi. (2008) Systemic therapy and attachment narratives. Systemic therapy and attachment narratives - Vetere - 2008 - Journal of Family Therapy - Wiley Online Library

104. Ibid.

105. Schore, Allan N. (2003) Affect Regulation and the Repair of the Self and Affect Dysregulation and Disorders of the Self. New York: W.W. Norton & Company. Pg 12

106. Flores, P. J. (2001). Addiction as an attachment disorder: Implications for group therapy. International Journal of Group Psychotherapie, 51, 63–81.

107. Ibid.

108. Ibid.

109. Flores, Philp. Addiction as an Attachment Disorder (2011) Jason Aronson, Inc. pg 7

110. Ibid.

111. Ibid.

112. The Reflective Functioning Questionnaire (RFQ) (Retrieved 2018) https://www.ucl.ac.uk/psychoanalysis/research/reflective-functioning-questionnaire-rfq

113. Hesse, E. (2008) The Adult Attachment Interview: Protocol, Method of Analysis, and Empirical Studies. In: Cassidy, J. and Shaver, P.R., Eds., Handbook of Attachment: Theory, Research, and Clinical Applications, 2nd Edition, Guilford Press, New York, 552-598.

114. Ibid.

115. Crowell, J., & Waters, E. (2005). Attachment Representations, Secure-Base Behavior, and the Evolution of Adult Relationships: The Stony Brook Adult Relationship Project. In K. E. Grossmann, K. Grossmann, & E. Waters (Eds.), *Attachment from infancy to adulthood: The major longitudinal studies* (pp. 223-244). New York, NY, US: Guilford Publications.

116. Hesse, E. (2008) The Adult Attachment Interview: Protocol, Method of Analysis, and Empirical Studies. In: Cassidy, J. and Shaver, P.R., Eds., Handbook of Attachment: Theory, Research, and Clinical Applications, 2nd Edition, Guilford Press, New York, 552-598.

117. Allen, J.G. (2006): *Mentalizing in practice*. In J.G. Allen & P. Fonagy (Eds.), Handbook of Mentalization-Based Treatment (pp. 3-26). Chichester: Wiley.

118. Fonagy, P., Gergely, G., Target, M., Jurist, Elliot L. (2005). Affect Regulation, Mentalization, and the Development of the Self. Other Press; 1 edition

119. Ibid.

120. Fonagy P, Target M. (1996) Playing with reality: I. Theory of mind and the normal development of psychic reality. Int Journal of Psychoanalyses. (Pt 2):217-33.

121. Ibid.

122. Fonagy P., Luyten P., Moulton-Perkins A, Lee YW, Warren F, Howard S, et al. (2016) Development and validation of a self-report measure of mentalizing: The Reflective Functioning Questionnaire. PLOS ONE. 11(7)

123. Brown, Daniel P., & Elliott, David S. (2016) in Attachment Disturbances in Adults. W. W. Norton & Company; pg 297

124. boyd, danah m. & Ellison, Nicole B. (2007) Social Network Sites: Definition, History, and Scholarship. *Journal of Computer-Mediated Communication*, Volume 13, Issue 1, Pages 210–230

125. Tracy, Elizabeth M., Whittaker, James K.(1990) The Social Network Map. Assessing Social Support in Clinical Practice. Families in Society, The Journal of Contemporary Human Services, Family Services of America.

126. Wallin, D. J. (2007). Attachment in Psychotherapy. New York, NY, US: Guilford Press.pg. 198.

127. Vetere, Arlene., Dallas, Rudi. (2008) Systemic therapy and attachment narratives. Systemic therapy and attachment narratives - Vetere - 2008 - Journal of Family Therapy - Wiley Online Library

APPENDIX

AIAT® Life areas assessment rating

How much are each of these areas a problem for you? Rate 0 – 5

0 = no problem, 1 = little problem, 2 = minor problem, 3 = somewhat of a problem, 4 = major problem, 5 = overwhelming problem H

How much alcohol or drug use contributes: Rate on 0-5 scale,

0 = no contribution, 1 = a little contribution, 2 = somewhat contributes, 3 = fair contribution, 4 = mostly contributes, 5 = completely contributes

How much psychiatric problems contribute

0 = no contribution, 1 = a little contribution, 2 = somewhat contributes, 3 = fair contribution, 4 = mostly contributes, 5 = completely contributes

Life area	How much of a	Substance Related	Mental Health Con-	Comments
Family relationships				
Spouse/partner				
Parenting				
Work				
Financial				
Physical Well-Being				
Emotional Well-				
Friendships				
Self-Esteem				
Spirituality				
Other (specify)				

Change Plan Worksheet

My current problem that I would like to address is:
The changes I would like to make related to this are:
The most important reasons why I want to make these changes are:

Resilience Assessment

Responses to Stressful Experiences Scale

The following statements describe how some individuals may think, feel, or act during and after the most stressful events in life. Please indicate how well each of these statements describes you during and after life's most stressful events.

4	3	2	1	0
Exactly Like Me				Not at All Like Me

During and after life's most stressful events, I tend to ...

...take action to fix things.

...not give up trying to solve problems I think I can solve.

...find a way to do what's necessary to carry on.

...pray or meditate.

...face my fears.

...find opportunity for growth.

...calm and comfort myself.

...try to "recharge" myself before I have to face the next challenge.

...see it as a challenge that will make me better.

...look at the problem in a number of ways.

...look for creative solutions to the problem.

...put things in perspective and realize I will have times of joy and times of   sadness.

...be good at determining which situations _are_ changeable and which _are not_.

...find meaning from the experience.

...find strength in the meaning, purpose, or mission of my life.

...know I will bounce back.

...expect that I can handle it.

...learn important and useful life lessons.

...understand that bad things can happen to anyone, not just me.

...lean on my faith in God or a higher power.

...draw upon lessons learned from failures and past mistakes.

...practice ways to handle it better next time.

Scoring and Algorithm

Note: For each assessment, there is a scoring algorithm leading to one of three acuity ranges: Low, moderate, high

Algorithm

Total = 71 – 88   High Resilience

Total = 50 – 70   Moderate Resilience

Total =   0 – 49   Low Resilience

Adapted for AIAT: The Reflective Functioning Questionnaire

Please work through the next 8 statements. For each statement, choose a number between 1 and 7 to say how much you disagree or agree with the statement, and write it beside the statement. Do not think too much about it – your initial responses are usually the best. Thank you.

Use the following scale from 1 to 7:

SCORING THE AIAT ADAPTED RFQ

The RFQ, used in the ABAT model, is to used for **general understanding** to gather a sense of a high or low ability to see the perspective and emotional state of others vs themselves. I have included the review of the RFQ tendencies for counselor scoring to draw a conclusion about the resident's ability to accurately understand themselves and others.

1. __ People's thoughts are a mystery to me (High number = Hypermentalizing)

2. __ I don't always know why I do what I do (High number = Hypomentalizing)

3. __ When I get angry I say things without really knowing why I am saying them (High number = Hypomentalizing)

4. __ When I get angry I say things that I later regret (High number = Hypermentalizing)

5. __ If I feel insecure I can behave in ways that put others' backs up (High number = Hypomentalizing)

6. __ Sometimes I do things without really knowing why (High number = Hypomentalizing)

7. __ I always know what I feel (High number = Hypermentalizing)

8. __ Strong feelings often cloud my thinking (High number = Hypermentalizing)

SOCIAL NETWORK DATA RECORDING SHEET

Names	1. Household 2.Family 3.Work/school 4.Support groups 5.Other friends 6.Neighbors 7.Professionals 8.Others	Concrete Support 1.Hardly ever 2.Sometime s 3. Almost always	Emotional Support 1.Hardly ever 2.Sometimes 3. Almost always	Inform./ Advice 1.Hardly ever 2 Some-times 3. Almost always	Critical 1.Hardly ever 2.Sometime s 3. Almost always	Direction Of Help 1.Goes both ways 2.You to Them 3. Them to You	Closeness 1.Hardly ever 2.Sometime s 3. Almost always	Often Seen 0.Never 1. Few times a year 2.Monthl y 3.Weekly 4.Daily	Time Known 1. less than a yr 2. 1-5 yr 3.More than 5 years
Example Mom	1, 2	3	2	3	2	3	2	4	3

Readiness Ruler

```
      0   1   2   3   4   5   6   7   8   9   10

      |   |   |   |   |   |   |   |   |   |   |

  Not ready for change                    Ready for change
```

On a scale of 1 to 10, how important is it to you to make a change in . . . ?

Example, If you are a 5, why are you a 5 and not a 3?

Or if you are a 5, what need to happen for you to go to a 7?

How could I assist you in getting to a 7?

Social Network Map

Date _____

YOU

Change Plan Worksheet

The change I want to make (or continue making) is:

The reason why I want to make this change is:

The steps I plan to take in changing are:

The ways other people can help me are:

I will know that my plan is working if:

Some things that could interfere with my plan are:

What I will do if the plan isn't working:

MIRC- Multidimensional Inventory of Recovery Capital Adapted for AIAT®

Based on research tool designed by Bowen, E. Irish, A. Wilding, G., LaBarre, C., Cappozziello, Nochajski, T. ,Granfield, R. & Kaskutas, L. (2023) MIRC- Multidimensional Inventory of Recovery Capital.

Name _____Date _____

Instructions: This survey asks how strongly you agree or disagree with each statement based on your current situation or how you feel right now. Your answers help identify resources and challenges in recovery. There e are no right or wrong answers.

Social Capital	1 Strongly Disagree	2 Disagree	3 Agree	4. Strongly Agree
I actively support other people who are in recovery				
My family makes my recovery more difficult				
I have at least one friend who supports my recovery				
My family supports my recovery				
Some people in my life do not think I'll make it in my recovery				
I feel alone.				
I feel like I am part of a recovery community				
Physical Capital				
My housing situation is helpful for my recovery.				
I have difficulty getting transportation.				
My housing situation is unstable.				
I have enough money each week to buy the basic things I need				
Not having enough money makes my recovery more difficult.				
I can afford the care I need for my health, mental health, and recovery.				
I have reliable access to a phone and the internet.				

Human Capital	1 Strongly Disagree	2 Disagree	3 Agree	4. Strongly Agree
I find it hard to have fun.				
I feel physically healthy most days.				
I am struggling with guilt and shame.				
I am experiencing a lot stress.				
My education and training have prepared me to handle life's challenges.				
I have problems with my mental health.				
I feel my life has purpose and meaning.				
Cultural Capital				
It's hard for me to trust others.				
I have opportunities to [participate in fun activities that do not involve drugs or alcohol.				
I feel disconnected from my culture or not part of any culture.				
I feel like an outcast.				
There are helpful services and resources available to me.				
It's hard to let go of the part of my identity that was linked to my drinking or drug sue.				
My neighborhood or town feels safe.				

Step One

What Is My Attachment Style?

The first step toward applying attachment theory to *your* life is to get to know yourself and those around you from an attachment perspective. In the next chapter, we'll walk you through the process of determining your partner or prospective partner's attachment style based on various clues. But let's begin by assessing the person you know best—yourself.

Which Attachment Style Am I?

Following is a questionnaire designed to measure your attachment style—the way you relate to others in the context of intimate relationships. This questionnaire is based on the Experience in Close Relationship (ECR) questionnaire. The ECR was first published in 1998 by Kelly Brennan, Catherine Clark, and Phillip Shaver, the same Shaver who published the original "love quiz" with Cindy Hazan. The ECR allowed for specific short questions that targeted particular aspects of adult attachment based on two main categories: anxiety in the relationship and avoidance. Later, Chris Fraley from the University of Illinois, together with Niels Waller and Kelly Brennan, revised the questionnaire to create the ECR-R. We present a modified version that we think works best in everyday life.

Attachment styles are stable but plastic. Knowing your specific attachment profile will help you understand yourself better and guide you in your interactions with others. Ideally this will result in more happiness in your relationships. (For a fully validated adult attachment questionnaire, you can log on to Dr. Chris Fraley's website at:
http://www.web-research-design.net/cgi-bin/crq/crq.pl.)

Check the small box next to each statement that is TRUE for you.
(If the answer is untrue, *don't* mark the item at all.)

	TRUE		
	A	**B**	**C**
I often worry that my partner will stop loving me.	☐		
I find it easy to be affectionate with my partner.		☐	
I fear that once someone gets to know the real me, s/he won't like who I am.	☐		
I find that I bounce back quickly after a breakup. It's weird how I can just put someone out of my mind.			☐
When I'm not involved in a relationship, I feel somewhat anxious and incomplete.	☐		
I find it difficult to emotionally support my partner when s/he is feeling down.			☐
When my partner is away, I'm afraid that s/he might become interested in someone else.	☐		

	TRUE		
	A	**B**	**C**
I feel comfortable depending on romantic partners.		☐	
My independence is more important to me than my relationships.			☐
I prefer not to share my innermost feelings with my partner.			☐
When I show my partner how I feel, I'm afraid s/he will not feel the same about me.	☐		
I am generally satisfied with my romantic relationships.		☐	
I don't feel the need to act out much in my romantic relationships.		☐	
I think about my relationships a lot.	☐		
I find it difficult to depend on romantic partners.			☐

	A	B	C
I tend to get very quickly attached to a romantic partner.	☐		
I have little difficulty expressing my needs and wants to my partner.		☐	
I sometimes feel angry or annoyed with my partner without knowing why.			☐
I am very sensitive to my partner's moods.	☐		
I believe most people are essentially honest and dependable.		☐	
I prefer casual sex with uncommitted partners to intimate sex with one person.			☐
I'm comfortable sharing my personal thoughts and feelings with my partner.		☐	

	TRUE		
	A	B	C
I worry that if my partner leaves me I might never find someone else.	☐		
It makes me nervous when my partner gets too close.			☐
During a conflict, I tend to impulsively do or say things I later regret, rather than be able to reason about things.	☐		
An argument with my partner doesn't usually cause me to question our entire relationship.		☐	
My partners often want me to be more intimate than I feel comfortable being.			☐
I worry that I'm not attractive enough.	☐		
Sometimes people see me as boring because I create little drama in relationships.		☐	
I miss my partner when we're apart, but then when we're together I feel the need to escape.			☐
When I disagree with someone, I feel comfortable expressing my opinions.		☐	
I hate feeling that other people depend on me.			☐

	A	B	C
If I notice that someone I'm interested in is checking out other people, I don't let it faze me. I might feel a pang of jealousy, but it's fleeting.		□	
If I notice that someone I'm interested in is checking out other people, I feel relieved — it means s/he's not looking to make things exclusive.			□
If I notice that someone I'm interested in is checking out other people, it makes me feel depressed.	□		
If someone I've been dating begins to act cold and distant, I may wonder what's happened, but I'll know it's probably not about me.		□	

	TRUE		
	A	**B**	**C**
If someone I've been dating begins to act cold and distant, I'll probably be indifferent; I might even be relieved.			□
If someone I've been dating begins to act cold and distant, I'll worry that I've done something wrong.	□		
If my partner was to break up with me, I'd try my best to show her/him what s/he is missing (a little jealousy can't hurt).	□		
If someone I've been dating for several months tells me s/he wants to stop seeing me, I'd feel hurt at first, but I'd get over it.		□	
Sometimes when I get what I want in a relationship, I'm not sure what I want anymore.			□
I won't have much of a problem staying in touch with my ex (strictly platonic) — after all, we have a lot in common.		□	

*Adapted from Fraley, Waller, and Brennan's (2000) ECR-R Questionnaire.

Add up all your checked boxes in column A: _____

Add up all your checked boxes in column B: _____

Add up all your checked boxes in column C: _____

Scoring Key

The more statements that you check in a category, the more you will display characteristics of the corresponding attachment style. Category A represents the *anxious attachment* style, Category B represents the *secure* attachment style, and Category C represents the *avoidant* attachment style.

Anxious: You love to be very close to your romantic partners and have the capacity for great intimacy. You often fear, however, that your partner does not wish to be as close as you would like him/her to be. Relationships tend to consume a large part of your emotional energy. You tend to be very sensitive to small fluctuations in your partner's moods and actions, and although your senses are often accurate, you take your partner's behaviors too personally. You experience a lot of negative emotions within the relationship and get easily upset. As a result, you tend to act out and say things you later regret. If the other person provides a lot of security and reassurance, however, you are able to shed much of your preoccupation and feel contented.

Secure: Being warm and loving in a relationship comes naturally to you. You enjoy being intimate without becoming overly worried about your relationships. You take things in stride when it comes to romance and don't get easily upset over relationship matters. You effectively communicate your needs and feelings to your partner and are strong at reading your partner's emotional cues and responding to them. You share your successes and problems with your mate, and are able to be there for him or her in times of need.

Avoidant: It is very important for you to maintain your independence and self-sufficiency and you often prefer autonomy to intimate relationships. Even though you do want to be close to others, you feel uncomfortable with too much closeness and tend to keep your partner at arm's length. You don't spend much time worrying about your romantic relationships or about being rejected. You tend not to open up to your partners and they often complain that you are emotionally distant. In relationships, you are often on high alert for any signs of control or impingement on your territory by your partner.

www.ingramcontent.com/pod-product-compliance
Lightning Source LLC
Chambersburg PA
CBHW020238290326
41929CB00044B/293